Nuanced Account Management

"An important book from a successful practitioner for everyone involved in B2B selling. The book tackles the important question of 'What drives competitive advantage in B2B sales?' It brings to center stage the importance of account management through practical guidance that will help every sales professional achieve their goals."
—Sanjiv Kakkar, *Executive Vice President, Unilever North Africa, Middle East, Turkey, Russia Ukraine and Belarus*

"Bala Shankar brings in his entire sales experience in this book in a very structured manner. Apart from his obsession on putting 'Customer' in the center of all your actions and strategies, Bala addresses the issues faced internally by an Account Manager in his/her organization and recommends how to maintain the right balance internally and externally."
—Anil Chugh, *Chief Executive, Consumer Care Business, Wipro, Bangalore, India*

"If you want to get to know best practices of B2B account management, sales effectiveness and customer engagement, this book is for you. Bala Shankar has done a wonderful job distilling key insights, tools, tactics and strategies. I love its practical and hands-on approach."
—Professor Jochen Wirtz, *Vice-Dean, Graduate Studies and Professor of Marketing, National University of Singapore (NUS), Singapore*

"Among the many important concepts Bala Shankar is sharing with the reader, the very key concept is to always 'sell benefits, not features,' While this seems trivial, it requires a fundamental mindset change."
—Professor Stefan Michel, *Dean of Executive MBA program and Faculty Representative, IMD Foundation Board, IMD, Lausanne, Switzerland*

Bala Shankar

Nuanced Account Management

Driving Excellence in B2B Sales

palgrave
macmillan

Bala Shankar
Management Consultant
Singapore, Singapore

ISBN 978-981-10-8362-4   ISBN 978-981-10-8363-1   (eBook)
https://doi.org/10.1007/978-981-10-8363-1

Library of Congress Control Number: 2018938122

Cover Illustration: © ikryannikovgmailcom / Getty Images

Printed on acid-free paper

This Palgrave Macmillan imprint is published by the registered company Springer Nature
Singapore Pte Ltd. part of Springer Nature.
The registered company address is: 152 Beach Road, #21-01/04 Gateway East, Singapore
189721, Singapore

Dedicated to the memory of my long-time boss and friend, Nick (Noubar Khoren) Hagop, who epitomized the best virtues of account management and was a generous mentor to me and to several generations of managers. Nick died of cancer in Brisbane, Australia, in May 2015.

PREFACE

Customer loyalty, customer delight and customer experience are salient concepts that are part of our marketing and sales vocabulary in the past decade or more. While they are more germane in a B2C (business to consumer) situation, we need a nuanced interpretation to be applied easily to the B2B (business to business) realm. In the B2B space, there is a dictum—selling more to an existing customer is more profitable (even up to ten times) than acquiring a new customer. Even assuming this is always true, it must be true for competition as well. Every company in an industrial space would thus want to sell more to existing customers. The B2B customer's wallet is often not that elastic. How do we therefore do it better than our competitors? Why would our customer treat us specially and favor us with more business, for longer periods of time? Can a vendor secure a large share (or even 100%) of a client's business? These are vital questions.

Bala Shankar

Acknowledgments

I have had the blessed privilege of working in an ecosystem that consisted of many bright and supportive colleagues, superiors and customers who shaped my thoughts and practice over the years.

I thank the several managers and entrepreneurs that I met in my customers' offices—perhaps more than 1000 and over 100 in just one building in Mumbai—who all played ball with me in my professional career and helped me learn and practice many lessons from the other side of the aisle, along the way. Their reciprocity was a key factor in my professional success and strengthened my belief in the concept, leading to penning this book. Many of them have been kind enough to browse my manuscript and give their candid opinions or endorsements. My senior colleagues were different in their mentoring styles. Besides Nick Hagop, who I have dedicated this book to, I would like to thank Changavalli Venkat and Roger Schmid, whose collegial support and creative freedom was important for my experiments and experiences. Many friends who are stalwarts in B2B industries and in the academia have been extremely kind to share their insights as I started to write.

My family has played its role in this project perfectly. My wife Alamelu, never one to interfere with my agenda, gave me the space and tacit approval to embark on this, often at the cost of my share of the family responsibilities. My daughter Rashmi, a psychology graduate, was my bouncing partner to help me link actions to behavioral concepts. My brother Venkatesh Shankar, Professor and Coleman Chair in Marketing at Mays Business School, Texas A&M University, and a researcher and prolific writer himself, who read my early drafts, gave me the encouragement to pursue writing on this subject. Lastly, my 81-year-old mother Rajalakshmi, silently proud of what I or my siblings do, deserves full credit for raising and educating us against several odds, ensuring our successful careers and our development of curious and persevering minds.

I would like to thank sincerely my charioteer, God, who played His invisible role in my transition from corporate career to entrepreneurship to teaching to now an author, opening these doors almost stealthily.

CONTENTS

CONTENTS

About the Author

Bala Shankar is a consultant and has been an adjunct marketing faculty at the School of business, Singapore Management University (SMU). A management graduate from the prestigious Indian Institute of Management (IIM), Ahmedabad, India, Bala has worked in Asia, Europe and the USA in various sales, account management and leadership capacities in a career spanning over 25 years. Bala held positions of Country Divisional Manager, Regional Director, Global Account Director and Global Sales program leader. Bala has been an adjunct faculty at various other universities and has been associated with executive development programs. He is a contributor to *The Business Times*, Singapore, on various business topics. Bala's leisure time is heavily invested in Indian classical music as lover, writer and critic. (Shankar.bala.s@gmail.com).

LIST OF FIGURES

LIST OF TABLES

CHAPTER 1

Introduction and Fundamentals

1.1 INTRODUCTION

'The total number of B2B sales jobs is more likely to grow than shrink over the next several years. In the modern economy, complexity and uncertainty aren't going away', wrote Andris A. Zoltners, PK Sinha and Sally E. Lorimer.[1] That's a piece of cheerful news, especially as it was cited in the context of relentless automation and artificial intelligence (AI) adoption. But we need to deal with the complexity and uncertainty mentioned. And we need to sell more. In the business-to-business (B2B) space, it is a well-accepted maxim that selling more to existing customers is more profitable than acquiring and selling to new customers. Depending on the source, it is believed that the profit differential between the two options is as much as seven to ten times. Given the enormity of this insight, companies often grapple with how to scale up activities with existing customers significantly and for a long period of time. Unable to implement a robust strategy in that direction, many companies continue to seek out scores of new customers, small and big, in order to fulfill top-line goals. That becomes their Plan A by default. What is a coherent sales approach that can deliver superior outcomes with existing customers? Can companies achieve (or even aim for) 100% share of their customers' wallets? How could companies

---

[1] Andris A. Zoltners, PK Sinha and Sally E. Lorimer, *Despite dire predictions, salespeople aren't going away* (*Harvard Business Review*, 31 March 2016).

© The Author(s) 2018
B. Shankar, *Nuanced Account Management*,
https://doi.org/10.1007/978-981-10-8363-1_1

1

build a competitive advantage landscape that is woven around this idea? These are interesting questions for which we seek answers here.

Concepts like customer loyalty, customer delight, customer experience and so on have flowered in the B2C (business-to-consumer) realm in the past years. Their parallel in B2B context is different and often measured in soft and ambiguous terms. What will constitute best practices that lead to a high customer satisfaction leading further to retention and realization of long-term customer value? This is the premise of this book.

I spent over 20 years in account management and sales leadership in a classic B2B industry (selling fragrances to consumer product companies like P&G, Unilever, Colgate and Johnson & Johnson). With four to five top suppliers in the industry serving almost all key customers, their stranglehold on customers was daunting for a non-player or a fringe player. My former company, although several decades old and somewhat strong in Europe, was trying to enter key Asian markets at that time, India being a prime focus. We had to devise different customer engagement and proximity strategies to overcome the non-incumbency disadvantage. In course of time, we converted it to an advantage. At the end of six years of aggressive deployment of the approach, the company achieved a market share of 18%, the highest by far. (This should be viewed in the context of 3–4% share that the company enjoyed globally.) My subsequent experiences in the company's global operations as well as after I moved into teaching and consulting, kept my interest in the subject of B2B account management alive. I came across some sterling examples of the powerful 'account management' approach as much as blissful ignorance of the tenets. These anecdotal experiences led to further insights that form the backbone of this book on *Nuanced Account Management*.

As I reflected on my experiences, a few things became clear. Our products were not unique, we had few special technologies, our prices were not cheaper, we were not among the top three players in most of the 70+ markets we operated in and our salesmen profile was about the same as competition, by and large. The natural question (indeed, for many of our competitors) was 'where is the competitive advantage?' It wasn't just one thing. What made the difference was the overall account management approach. By shifting the center of gravity to the management of customers in a comprehensive way, we positioned ourselves with a clear point of difference. Customers often gave us a seat in boardroom discussions and shared long-term plans. We fine-tuned the approach with every day, every customer meeting, every success and every failure.

The multiple touchpoints that the business inherently offers enriched the cumulative learning that settled into a virtuous pattern. These experiences in account management have driven my interest in the subject to an evangelical degree, manifesting in this book.

As readers would notice in the ensuing chapters, there is no single silver bullet or a 'eureka' moment in this. It is a bulwark of several inter-related strategies, tactics and skillsets that account teams and leaders need to consistently deploy in order to realize the outcomes. Once connected, the dots present the holistic picture of account management. Adding continuously to real and perceived value for customers is the hallmark of a top supplier. It is not a quick-fix strategy either. The benefits are long term and so is the labor—it's long-distance running. Some of the ideas are simple and well known (and yet may not be adopted diligently) while the others are deeper interpretations. For some companies and managers, this book may be a further assurance of their customer intimacy and engagement strategy. For many others, it may prompt a radical shift in approach.

Account management is not new. But the understanding and application are varied. Further, its contours are undergoing vast changes. As customers seek more and more from suppliers and even to the extent of demanding them to be stakeholders, every small step to endear to them is vital. Competition gets bigger and tougher while product and service advantages keep shrinking. A powerful coagulation of account management practice is, thus, an investment toward a higher order competitive advantage, not easy to replicate. The book drives that message, with its over 40 ideas.

It is still mistakenly believed that good account management is all about networking, socializing, personal affinity between the salesperson and the buyer, smart-talking and playing 'Mandrake'. That is not just mythical but is grossly unfair to the professionalism and caliber of buying teams and their companies. Buying is now a specialist career and the professionals are often trained for relevant skills (just as salesmen are trained to sell). People who are called 'smart salespeople' are, in fact, the best practitioners of all the lessons in this book. It may be just that they carry their skillsets without advertising them.

The concepts in this book matter more than ever. We are living through a revolution that brings machines close to human areas of work—driverless cars, robots, process automation, artificial intelligence (AI), technology enablers, internet of things (IoT) and so on. It is tempting to imagine that selling and marketing may be part of the next frontiers. (Some customer relationship management (CRM) systems almost allude to that scenario.) That will not happen. Human touchpoints in business will move into a higher plane where machines cannot substitute. The complexity of the buyer-seller dynamics in B2B will ensure that 'people' continue to be the anchor for business success. The World Economic Forum, in its most in-demand professions in 2016,[2] lists sales at number four (after nursing, app development and marketing), ahead of many technology jobs. The list is measured based on the gap between supply and demand. While that should be great news, the people (in sales and account management) will need to upgrade skills, tools, nuanced strategies and competitive ideas to keep and grow the distance. Re-scripting the account management code and bringing it into the spotlight is thus important. The anecdotal references cover many industries that I have been associated with in my work, consulting and project coaching experiences—consumer packaged goods (CPG) fast moving consumer goods (FMCG) ingredients, IT services, banking, medical technologies, market research services and so on.

The basic aspects of selling are not covered in the book. The several 'golden rules' expounded as a more nuanced approach envelop the following seven broad categories:

Tactics and approaches for sales effectiveness
Strategies for deep customer engagement
Skillsets and knowledge (of account teams)
Proactive relationship management
Organizational and human resource imperatives
Customer Innovation bias
Pitfalls to avoid

1.2   ACCOUNT MANAGEMENT

Account Management refers to the sum of all activities that contribute toward acquiring and servicing a customer in the B2B space aimed at long-term sustenance of business and profitability. It is normally referred to in the context of 'industrial marketing' or B2B marketing where the customer is a corporate, institution or a government organization and is not an individual. Account management is equally relevant in product or service industries and in product plus service contexts. It has common codes with 'sales', 'business development', 'customer relationship' or 'client servicing'

[2] *Most in-demand jobs for 2016* (World Economic Forum, December 2015).

activities, but there are some crucial differences that necessitate a more nuanced and refined approach from vendors. Some of these *differences* (including some well-established ones) are captured below:

1. The customers are usually repeat buyers and have the potential to buy the same product/service or similar range of products/services again. In some cases, there may be several repeat buys of the same product.
2. The pre-sales to post-sales cycle is long and can stretch to multi-years for individual projects or contracts.
3. A team of people are involved on the customer's side playing different roles like influencing, evaluating, recommending and decision-making. They also represent varied functions and hierarchies and carry their own diverse objectives.
4. The buying process is complex and involves multiple steps, and may include back-and-forth movements. The process may have several milestones and interim fulfillment stages.
5. The buying criteria are complex and will include stated and unstated considerations.
6. The buying criteria may include a combination of quantitative, qualitative and judgmental factors.
7. The pricing considerations could consist of multiple layers of unit price, volume discounts, performance bonus (or penalties), guaranteed cost savings, cost sharing and royalties (for exclusivity).
8. The customer relationships at the organizational level can last very long, sometimes to perpetuity. It can thus last beyond the tenures of many managers.
9. Buyers are normally very well informed of all matters relating to the item of purchase and selling organizations play a part in the knowledge transfer process.
10. Buyers deal with several competing vendors at the same time and can develop a good mastery of all information and issues relating to the product or service.
11. The buying maybe centralized for a large number of divisions or geographical units of a corporate.
12. The selling organization is also often the source of new ideas, process and product innovation, research, analysis, related technologies, market insights and so on.

13. Depending upon the industry, values of contracts can go up to hundreds of millions of dollars.
14. The customer demand is often inelastic—a price reduction will not lead to increase in the buying quantity.
15. Pre-qualification of vendors maybe built into the process, both in government as well as in the private sector.
16. Competition and co-operation with customers may co-exist simultaneously.
17. Purchase contracts may include post-sales services and commitments like maintenance, upgradation, performance assurance, replacement and upgrade.
18. Purchase contracts may include exclusivity clauses and arrangements and rights for usage of proprietary technologies and patents.
19. Due to the long tenure of the business or contracts, price variation clauses are usually integral to the terms.
20. Purchase contracts may or may not have 'end of contract' terms. Thus contracts may be rolled over automatically (unless terminated).
21. Vendors may choose to do business with only a select list of customers; similarly, customers may deal with only select vendors.
22. The legal and commercial complexity of contracts can be enormous and may need involvement of specialists.

Examples Where Account Management Is Relevant
For the sake of completeness, (even though it should be obvious), a few typical examples of B2B sales situations (not exhaustive) are: ingredient/raw material sales to a pharmaceutical manufacturer; sale or lease of aircraft to an airline; sale of medical equipment to a hospital or the government; sale of telecast rights by a producer to a television broadcaster; offer of construction services to the government (for roads, bridges, etc.); sale of software applications or hardware to a corporate or an institution; corporate banking services; third-party manufacture contract with a brand owner; supply of equipment or parts to a manufacturer or wholesaler or retailer; offer of insurance services to a corporate or a government body; sale of military/defense equipment to a government or an organization; commodity or other ingredient supply to a processor; back office support services provided to a corporate or a government body/department; supply of merchandise to a super- or hyper-market chain; consulting, audit, architectural, legal or due diligence services provided to a

corporate or an institution or to a government department; channel selling arrangements between a manufacturer and a reseller or a distributor; annual maintenance contracts between a service provider and corporates or institutions; supply arrangements between an online retailer and product or service providers; logistics, supply chain and aggregation services offered to corporates and institutions … the list is endless.

Let us study in a nutshell the contrasting way in which customers are served in a conventional sales organization and in an account management structure. In the traditional sales organizations, territory is the main unit of focus. Thus teams are divided and given geographical areas to look after. The customers therefore come with the territory. A customer, with different branch or factory operations in different parts of a nation or the world, is served like a local customer by a local team. In a few cases, customers may be linked to a salesperson by being part of the 'same' business or product line, irrespective of size or importance. By contrast, integrated national, regional or global account management provides a 'single window' service to a customer. Thus the customer is the unit of sales strategy (not products, services, business lines or geographies). An account manager typically 'owns' one or more customers, depending on the size and complexity of the business.

Whether the situation is a local, national, regional or global one, the inventory of best practices in the following chapters recognizes the above differences and can collectively and in an interlocked way provides an effective umbrella solution to the challenge. It is not necessary that a company should practice 'account management' for all its accounts. A prudent mix of account management for priority or strategic customers and general sales approach for the others may be the winning formula with focus on optimizing resources and marrying horses for the courses. Siemens, the global powerhouse in technology and services, has this hybrid arrangement: 'Approximately a million business-to-business customers are served globally by 430,000 Siemens employees, of which 40,000 are in sales, with the number of account managers at more than 2000.'[3] Some companies make a distinction between 'qualified' prospects or opportunities and the rest, to determine the depth of account management engagement required. However, as companies gravitate towards the larger and more

---

[3] *Siemens: Account management at a technology company,* (Velocity Reprint, Vol. II No. 1 1stquarter 2009).

important or valuable customers, they would find that these concepts have to be applied to a very large part of their business and maybe the whole of it. This will need a systemic commitment, embedding the principles in the process and sustained build-up of skillsets. It therefore follows that the subtle differences between 'key account selling' and 'strategic account management' that some management literature refer to are more semantic than significant.

While assessing the role of the account management team, it would be clear from the later chapters that the circumference of this role is constantly expanding. New skills, new ideas of services, new customer endearment measures are invented regularly, both by vendors and by customers, setting new benchmarks every time.

In the past couple of decades, channel partners have become a significant extension to the sales organization of many technology, equipment and appliance companies. Some of these channel partners are very large. This presents a unique situation whereby companies practice account management vis-à-vis the channel partners on the one side and, in co-operation with the same channel partners, perform a similar role with the ultimate institutional customers. Channel partners are thus customers, competitors (as they may trade a range of brands) and co-opetitors in the same breath. Account management is a key pivot to the success of this model as it builds long-term advantages in a scenario of nebulous market relationships.

There is a mistaken notion that account management has more utility in situations involving customized products and solutions rather than in standardized product-marketing scenarios (including commodities). As would be evident from many of the key lessons delineated in the book, account management is an inescapable tool to be mastered in all circumstances. In fact, it may even have a better pay-off in commoditized businesses, as there is little else that can be differentiated.

Impact of Digital Trends

The advent of digital and online platforms and practices has impacted the account management perspective in a few ways. In areas like sharing of information with customers or prospects, prospect qualification, lead generation, supply chain tracking, project tracking, transactional analysis and so on, internet and computing technologies have been greatly helpful in automating, providing real-time data and seamless information experience to customers. It is even possible that customers are well into the buying process before they start the interaction with the account teams.

However, CRM is not account management. In the core functions of engaging the customer, convincing the customer, building, maintaining and deepening relationships and creating long-term loyalty, account management cannot be digitized. Further, as all automated processes can be replicated by competition, nuanced high performance account management practiced by a team of specialists is the only avenue to stay differentiated. Companies need to adopt a judicious mix of digital and human interface with customers that optimizes the two capabilities.

1.3   What Do B2B Customers Want?

In a simplistic sense, customers want products or services for which they are willing to pay a price. However, the advent of technology and modern-day business processes has shaped the needs dramatically in recent decades. These impinge heavily on vendors. What specific ways can a customer's needs manifest? How are these articulated, if at all? It is useful to understand the broadest multi-dimensional suite of buyer needs in B2B scenarios before we try to make sense out of how the lessons leading to nuanced account management could be applied. The needs articulated here are generic in nature and can be contextualized easily. Refer to Table 1.1 for a summary picture.

Value

Buyers seek value in all situations. Value is not narrowly defined as price per unit or overall cost of the buy. It is a complex combination of all benefits versus all cost incurred or to be incurred (together with the financial implications of commercial terms) over the life of the product or service they would use. Value is generally quantifiable in dollar terms and in

Table 1.1   B2B customer 'wants' spectrum

Rational	Emotional	Professional
Value	Reliability	Enhancing competitiveness
Quality	De-risking	Innovation
Time	Ease of buying	Ideas
Solution to problems	Care and concern	Information
Customization	Participation	Strategic fit
Support services	Contribution to personal goals	Consulting advice
	Soft objectives	Soft objectives

terms of ratios like ROI. Value is also time-sensitive. There are short-term value needs and long-term value needs. A unique characteristic of the B2B industry is 'switching costs' which refers to costs incurred for changing from supplier A to supplier B or from product A to product B. This can be a significant barrier. Buyers thus decide the precise metric of what constitutes value for their buy.

Time

Customers are highly sensitive to the time taken for buying and implementation, leading up to the date they can start using the product or service. The time sensitivity is more accentuated if the buy is linked to a go-to-market plan. The challenge is more complicated by the long processes, multiple steps, multiple role-players, scope changes, price changes and decision delays. Timely fulfillment is also impacted by intermediate completion or delivery deadlines.

Quality

This is a parameter that over time has become a given thing and non-negotiable. Nevertheless, customers specify in detail, the quality requirements, both hard measures and soft aspects. There are two components to quality—the industry standard and the customer-specific expectations which may be more stringent. Vendors are expected to comply with both. In recent decades, the tolerance for quality deviation is also measured in terms of 'sigma' defects. In service industries, quality is often a mixture of quantitative and qualitative parameters (e.g. warm welcome greeting).

Reliability

From product and service reliability, there is a gradual metamorphosis to organizational reliability in modern buyer-seller relationships. Thus factors like personal reliability, financial reliability and price reliability have been added to transactional reliability.

Solutions to Problems

At the heart of buying and selling is the objective to solve problems—apparent and hidden, articulated and unarticulated, current and future, rational and emotional. Thus vendors have the responsibility to diagnose problems comprehensively and to address them. The product or service is thus only a means to the end goal of solving a problem comprehensively. In another sense, the business of a vendor is 'solving customers' problems' rather than selling something.

Enhancing Competitiveness

Customers often have a competitive goal to be fulfilled by buying a product or a service. It could range from marketplace superiority vis-à-vis competitors to internal advantages like staff retention or cost efficiencies to metrics like corporate and brand reputation. In some situations, customers may even seek 'exclusive' competitive advantage (usually for a period of time) through the purchase of a product or a service.

De-risking

A buyer also desires to de-risk his or her company from consequences of the various kinds of potential risks and buying mistakes like timing, appropriateness, cost, scope and technology. The implication is that buyer will be anxious to secure assurances to this effect and sellers don the role of risk-bearers and may be expected to accept recourse terms and consequences.

Customization

In many industries, there is a certain degree of customization involved. Customers and vendors have opposing goals in this aspect. Vendors would like to do the least amount of customization and buyers would seek full tailoring. Bridging the gap effectively and consensually is imperative. There is usually a cost implication depending on the extent of customization.

Innovation

A new buy is seldom a mere one-to-one replacement to the status quo. The genesis of a buying opportunity may itself be to seek an improvement, incremental or disruptive. Thus buyers want to embrace innovative products and services. This would include cutting-edge technologies and solutions or research ideas yet to be commercialized. Buyers are now known to outsource a significant part of their business innovation to vendors, not just to save cost and time but also to broaden the fountain of ideas.

Ideas

Customers see vendors as a source of new ideas to solve their business problems, even those unrelated to the product or service offered by a vendor. A strong vendor-customer relationship could lead to vendors acting as 'unpaid advisors' beyond their core business. Customers may expect this from vendors, merely by the fact that they have visibility of best practices in the industry and maybe from other industries. Customers also view this as a symbol of 'shared' ownership of business fortunes.

Information

Customers have a voracious appetite for information—everything under the sun as far as the vendor's products, businesses and competition are concerned. Their managers are, in some ways, consumers of information. They expect the vendors to be the 'credible' source even though internet and other public sources are available. The range and depth of information have expanded vastly in recent decades, as buyers try to garner the same level of expertise as the vendors. Precision and specificity define the quality of information expected from vendors.

Ease of Buying

The pangs of buying are another source of anxiety for buyers. It could relate to the product or the service, the costs, the time, the internal journey and coordination, implementation, commercial terms, disruption to the operating routines and more. The whole process can be exhausting and debilitating. Thus buyers seek to go through a simple, painless process that does not leave any scars. One important development, as a corollary, is that buyers farm out a good part of the buying process back to the sellers, including areas like need articulation, developing solution architecture, onboarding process for the new solution and so on. With the transfer of responsibility comes the challenge to smoothen the process of pre-buying, buying and post-buying. Thus the vendor's sales process has got extended in order to serve the 'ease' of buying goals. Vendors are often expected to assist the buyer navigate through evaluation of alternative solutions as well.

Care and Concern

The engagement is usually very long, lasting several months or years and going beyond several teams and perhaps generations. Sellers need to show adequate care and concern during this period, in normal times as well as when there is turbulence. This aspect draws from the human nature of the relationships that underpin the engagement even if we would tend to think that commercial basis is the one that drives the engagement. An organization is made up of its people and their emotional needs and wants. The different forms of care and concern would be determined by the strength of the relationships and the need of the situation.

Participation

An important unarticulated desire of the buyers is to actively and meaningfully participate in the buying. They do not like to be 'sold' or feel hoodwinked even remotely. They need to be taken into confidence, provided with relevant knowledge and insights and guided through the process. They like to own the process and the decision and want the satisfaction of being in charge. This is a subtle emotional need that many salesmen may miss, as it is never articulated in so many words.

Contribution to Personal Goals

People are the faces of customers we deal with and they have personal goals and aspirations. It could take the form of 'ushering in change' or 'dramatic improvements in performance' or 'solving a stubborn problem that many people tried and failed'. The managers involved may stake their reputation on the purchase in order to achieve these goals. This requires that the vendor assists the managers to achieve that personal goal, both from the vendor's company and from the sales teams. It demands sensitivity to recognize such a need and respond to it.

Strategic Fit

Corporate and institutional customers often desire a strategic fit between themselves and the vendors they choose as 'strategic suppliers'. The fit, like a marriage, could be based on factors like size, leadership position in the respective industries, geographic capabilities, financial strength, compatibility of business practices, quality of people and stage of organizational development, and may also include aspects relating to ownership and senior management. Short-term and long-term priorities of the two sides are also built into the strategic fit analysis.

Support Services

Several B2B businesses have a vital post-sales service component. The range of these services and the mode of delivering them have undergone a sea change. With technology platforms, customers can now have their own portal space with capability to view a variety of transactional, historical and forward-looking information as well as to request new services and to track pending service requests or update pertinent information electronically on a self-service basis. Initially introduced by the technology industry, this is now embraced by most industries.

Consulting Advice

Many buyers seek consulting support and advice before, during and after a buy. The scope of support could include situational analysis, diagnosis of problems, technology or solution options, cost information, market studies, project feasibility and more. This responsibility has seamlessly moved into the scope of vendors, from buyer-appointed consultants. Post-implementation surveys and analysis are further extensions. The key aspect to note is that these are normally offered 'free' as additional passport to securing or staying in an opportunity. Vendors therefore find it challenging to limit such 'free' services.

Soft Objectives

Buyers have softer and ethical objectives like personal reliability, transparency, truth, acting in good faith, acting in their interest, honesty in communication, relationship governance, trust, confidentiality and copyright compliance. This can extend to issues like child labor avoidance, animal testing, carbon footprint, gender equality, sustainable practices and diversity quotient. These are expected from both the organization and the individuals representing it. Most of these are unstated (or unamplified) and therefore the degrees are subject to interpretation. The onus is on the vendors to gauge these and the levels demanded.

We thus observe that everything is not reduced to dollars and cents. Customers have a holistic character and this manifests itself in many diverse needs, wants and wishes. Besides the usual rational category, there are also the 'emotional' needs (like the retail consumer) and an organizational/professional wish-list which is a category by itself. Many of these have to be discovered during the journey of engagement with the customer. 'Business buyers seek different benefit bundles based on their stage in the purchase decision process'—Philip Kotler.[4]

The modern-day B2B customer is also evolving rapidly in terms of deep in-house knowledge and in building a challenging array of expectations and barriers. This bar is being raised continuously. Vendors are assigned scores along multiple dimensions. Sales teams, however, often lag behind in fully comprehending this and see the relationship completely through the commercial and transactional prisms.

From questions like 'Who owns the sale?' or 'Who owns the customer?', we have decisively moved into the more customer-centric view of 'Who owns the customer experience?' One word has thus expanded the perspective with which we need to approach customers in B2B space.

While the general list of needs and desires is enumerated in no particular order of importance, the account management toolkit for each customer would depend on the relative ranking and weightages of these for that specific customer. Account management teams must configure the 'buyer demand' list before deciding the combination of the key lessons that would merit more considered application for each customer. The added complexity for global customers is that different parts of the organization may exhibit different need sets. Technology keeps ushering in changes to these requirements at a rapid pace. The most striking development in B2B is the facility to place orders via apps and the tracking systems possible across devices. As the wish list keeps changing, it is vital that vendors periodically review and update the list.

In the ensuing chapters and sub-chapters, a number of steps are delineated that would serve as a composite basket for achieving the sales and customer goals of a B2B enterprise.

---

[4] Philip Kotler, *Marketing Management*, tenth edition (Prentice Hall), pp. 192–215.

CHAPTER 2

Tactics and Approaches for Sales Effectiveness

2.1 SELL BENEFITS, NOT FEATURES

How is your product or service presented to potential customers, as a standard approach? Do the sales teams have a good understanding of what benefit(s) matters to each customer? Does your account team fully comprehend the difference between benefits and features?

*The intelligent marketers of today don't sell products, they sell benefits packets. Not only do **they sell purchase** value but also **usage value**—*Philip Kotler, legendary pioneer of marketing concepts.[1]

In the B2B space, customers are very clear about the distinction between benefits and features. If you are buying a polycarbonate roofing system for your open quadrangle, its compressive strength and the yellowing index are not the baits but its lightweight durability versus other options like glass, its high impact resistance, its effective light transmission as well as energy saving compared to other equivalents may be the winning package of benefits that you are willing to pay for. We always come across sales arguments that befuddle this distinction and therefore the opportunity to

[1] Philip Kotler, *Marketing Management*, tenth edition (Prentice Hall), 192–215.

© The Author(s) 2018
B. Shankar, *Nuanced Account Management*,
https://doi.org/10.1007/978-981-10-8363-1_2

drive home the advantage is lost. This is not just because the salesman's standard script is not clearly written. It is often due to the misplaced enthusiasm of the salesman to project his talents or his knowledge that clouds his thinking for what matters to a customer. It may also be due to insufficient knowledge of each customer's unique usage processes or end applications and benefits needs. This results in standardized catalogues and printed materials or online product data that focus inadequately on benefits.

In a B2C situation, this is differently practiced and is worth a quick look. We as buyers of, say, consumer electronics are expected to go through pages of catalogues and decipher the benefits more appropriate to us. We need to learn about HDMI cables and what device connections they help establish, for example. I have been sold 'radial' tires many times as part of my cars, without anyone ever telling me how they help (I appropriated them for better grip, safety or tire life). In B2B, the customer expects to hear the benefits narrated to him, ideally in his order of interest and in unambiguous terms. There must be a coherent story (we will talk in detail about storytelling in a later chapter) on benefits, the nature and in some cases the degree or the extent. (You could say that the light reflection of polycarbonate is about 95% as efficient as glass.) In some instances, the benefits will be a comparative study to the customer's next best (or more common) alternative.

Our account management team was trained to obtain key 'needs' information from each of their customers, rank the priorities, line them up against a checklist and then prepare the sales pitch according to this information. The benefit matrix was often tailored to each customer even though it was carved out of a general inventory. Pack sizes, for instance, were not relevant to large customers, who could handle bulk packaging, while the smaller customer, who had manual material handling operations, preferred smaller packs. Some customers also insisted on full quality control documents of their supply batches as they had to conform to traceability norms or external certification of their own processes, while the others did not care. Some needed our product to be performance-stable in adverse chemical or thermal processing and storage conditions while others did not have such difficult threshold. Some products needed fragrances that last long after product use (floor cleaners) while in others, longevity was not as critical as diffusion during use.

Our products had another inherent difficulty. The main reasons why products were chosen related more to emotional (sensorial, feel-good, relatable, unique, mood-appropriate, likable) factors than hard specifications. In this respect, they are similar to art pieces, beauty or gourmet food products. Articulating emotional connections of a fragrance to a consumer or market need is the 'benefit' suite that our customers expected. The fact that a certain type of ingredient from Madagascar was used in a new creation did not carry as much weight as describing the resultant mood-connect or the surrogate association to a functional or aesthetic benefit.

I have been at the other end of the spectrum trying to buy computer hardware on behalf of organizations. I have seldom heard a good story of why a certain switch is preferable over another for companywide LAN network or why firewall X is more suited to our requirements as compared to firewall Y. The latest confusion is with cloud applications and disaster recovery solutions. The fact that many of the sales teams for these products are from channel partners (who may be smaller companies) and not the equipment or software makers can complicate this further. You are never sure if you made the right choice since the benefit arguments were not well presented. I am not clear if this happens because salesmen have more comfort in talking the specification language or if companies truly have not spent time in articulating benefits well.

The feature-benefit distinction is not new. However, organizations need to build an awareness of their customers' benefit 'wish-list' into their standard sales narratives and train the account management team to develop appropriate scripts and practice them rigorously. The default language needs to be benefits-led.

In complex systems like medical electronics for hospitals and production equipment used in factories, different customer departments have different benefit needs. The finance needs the capital cost and operating cost (compared to other possible options); the technician or the operator needs throughput rates, electricity consumption, ease of use and so on; the maintenance crew needs cost of spare parts, service turnaround time and warranty, among others; and the head of the unit may need lead time for delivery and installation. All of these benefits need to be incorporated into the product deck offered to a customer.

Projecting Benefits on Faceless Media

In the modern-day scenario, some of the pre-sales engagement happens via faceless modes like website, portals, electronic direct mails (EDMs) and online client forums. The same rule of benefits versus features applies to this as well. This is perhaps even more critical considering that websites and other such modes tend to have a huge volume of information (an omnibus approach for all kinds of prospects and customers) that do not provide a 'distilled' benefits view. All content that are made available in these channels must have clear statements made on benefits that customers will enjoy with specific products and models. In the open era of information, this would also mean that your competitive secrets (of benefits) are available for competitors to see. One way to mitigate this would be a combination of generic or first order benefits being posted on faceless public channels and the more differentiated and higher order benefits being reserved for face-to-face meetings of account teams. Presenting the right mix of general data (for first-time viewers) and analyzed, segmented data (for repeat or enlightened customers) in websites or EDMs is a subject by itself (online content management), well explored in many quarters.

What Do You Sell?

The next logical question is what do you really sell to a B2B customer? Is it products, services or solutions? Is it solutions or your insight, knowledge, credibility and trust that make you uniquely competent to solve the customer's problems? Enlightened organizations reckon that it is their unique expertise and commitment that are offered to customers. Solutions, products, services or benefits are derivatives of that expertise and commitment. Therefore, even before solutions are offered, an account manager would need to earn his/her and his/her organization's stripes. The benefits that reflect your reputation are different from benefits that are derived from using your products or services. Tata Consultancy Services (TCS), a leading software company, uses the tag-word 'certainty' while describing their services in their corporate advertisement. That is a very powerful statement of benefit derived by buying from them (not products, not staff strength, not worldwide offices, not proprietary technologies and not specific knowledge).

The next time you introduce a new product in the market, do this exercise: Create two sets of sales information (literature, brochure, audio-visual, online content), one containing features and specifications and the other containing only the benefits. Offer the benefit story first to customers to see their response. You may be surprised that many customers never even ask about the features, or only to a minor extent, after exhausting the discussions on benefits. It is a great way to train the salesmen to speak that language as well, as a habit.

Some companies have developed a model whereby the sales kit has just benefits while features are covered through an FAQ (frequently asked questions) page that the customer can self-read for his or her understanding, if it is of interest. (In some situations, operating or technical departments may need the specifications and features, but the deciding authorities are often more interested in the benefits.)

2.2   PUT YOURSELF IN THE SHOES OF THE BUYER

Does your sales team think on behalf of the customer? Do they reflect the ocular of the customer in designing strategies and sales approaches? Is there an institutional mechanism in your organization to reflect voice of the customer at the pre-sales and during sales stages?

It is a common complaint that sales teams are not fully empathetic to the customer and his or her needs. This concept tries to take the issue one step further. If you think like the customer, you can address questions like what would be his priorities, what are his constraints, how much will the customer encourage you, what does he feel about your company's capabilities, what will be the nature of conversations he is likely to have with your company, what could be his objections and more. Experts in Poker or Game theory know this aspect of play very well. We are not just talking about hard facts of the customer but the soft underlying perspectives that could govern the engagement between your company and the customer that could swing deals either way. As discussed in Sect. 1.3, buyers' wants include emotional and professional bucket lists, some of which are not even articulated.

If you think like the customer from the beginning, you may even 'create' a sales opportunity that did not exist yet. '[I]nsight sales is the idea of showing up and not asking the customer what is keeping you up at night, but actually telling them what should be keeping them up at night. And obviously, doing it in a very empathetic kind of way, but the idea is teaching customers about business opportunities and problems, often, ideas of the customer, him or herself, hasn't even thought of before, so new ways to save money, or make money, or avoid risk over the horizon that the customer have even thought of and educating the customer about those problems which then ultimately lead to the things that you can deliver better than the competition.'[2]

Sales teams often imagine the relationship to be adversarial where one party is trying to out-smart the other and hence feel the urge to pull out all combat techniques. It is hard for a salesperson to fully identify with the customer, in view of such prejudiced attitude. Why can't the salesmen put themselves in the shoes of the buyer? After all, they are in the buyers' situation often, either as individuals or as managers representing the buying team in their company. The psychology of buyers and how it manifests in buying interactions or decisions is a critical subject for sales teams to comprehend and apply.

We trained and encouraged the sales team to advance the customer's likely viewpoints and objections in internal meetings. This was, of course, never intended to create 'excuses' for potential deal losses but as a constructive opportunity to build arguments that would counter and manage customer viewpoints. In our training sessions, we even had role-plays with our staff playing customer roles and simulating conversations as advocates of customers. In some ways, this is akin to preparing a set of FAQs (questions from the customer and potential answers of the vendor).

Voice of the Customer

One of the essential ingredients to this approach is the acknowledgment that customers will normally give you a fair chance, provided their viewpoints are understood and their concerns addressed genuinely. This understanding has to be established over time. 'Voice of the customer' is a powerful notion but it takes two to tango. For the customer to open up and voice their concerns, account teams have the obligation to create the right tone of engagement. At the slightest indication of unfair rebuttal or unsatisfactory answers, customers may retreat to a shell and curtail the openness. This is obviously not desirable. Therefore, genuine empathy has to be shown. Account managers' natural instinct is to devalue customer opinions and characterize them as a symptom of negotiation ploy. In my several relationships with customers, this was hardly the case. A mature view of customers' ocular is a useful skill to cultivate. I have also found that many times customers express opinions (or pose questions) based on their interaction with our competitors. This is thus a good source of getting a

---

[2] *The new sales playbook: An interview with Matt Dixon* (*Harvard Business Review*, 2012).

full view of the competitive landscape and dynamics. When customers ask questions or express concerns, they are giving us information. Team leaders of account managers should also encourage their team to present customer viewpoints and not to brand these as sales 'excuses'.

One of the incisive trainers we frequently engaged, Mercuri Goldmann India,[3] a company in the Mercuri International Group, would often have a session on 'emptying the customer'. The concept revolved around asking the customer 'what are your concerns—help us understand them?' This is a simple but powerful question. Some customers will pour out theirs including some tough ones, but many will also respect the willingness to embrace and address concerns. This question, if asked at the right stage of the sales process, can ensure that there are no surprises as we try to close in on a deal. Salesmen are usually reticent about asking this question for fear of being unable to address them and jeopardize a potential deal. They need to be trained to field these questions with objective answers. It is also a good skill that will help manage 'naysayers' in the customer organization, even before objections surface.

Price discussion, for example, can be traumatic for some people. It is the customer's duty to raise a price concern, even if you are the cheapest. Purchase managers are often paid for savings achieved from previous purchases or get their brownie points for slashing prices from quotations. It is equally the salesman's right to defend the price and not be apologetic about it, when it is fair. Putting yourself in the customer's shoes and examining the price situation from his angle can provide the right clues to the stand you want to take or the arguments you would like to present. Preparing the right logic can achieve more predictable price outcomes. I am not a votary of the theory that some salespeople have a natural skill to counter such situations. Even if some do, they will have a better outcome if they can anticipate customer questions and concerns.

If the buying terrain is correctly judged, it will also provide advance notice to shore up the sales arguments. Our emphasis on taking the customer's perspective often helped us to 'realistically' assess our chances in a project. If we concluded that our chances were weak, it goaded our teams to devise additional reinforcements to enhance our side of the arguments. If you are overconfident and fail to see the obstacle, it may spell a negative outcome.

---

[3] www.mercuriindia.com, October 2017.

Besides through specific training, this skill builds up with exposure. If practiced over a few customers, over a few cycles, account managers will be able to accurately 'anticipate' views of the customer and plan responses to those. In companies where different account managers deal with different customers in the same industry segment, it is an ideal opportunity to encourage collaboration for such tasks, as many issues are likely to be common. This could therefore be converted to an organizational capability rather than just being an individual skill.

In your next training program for sales teams, include a session of role-plays between the customer and your salesman with a no-holds-barred brief for the person playing the customer part. This would drive the salesman to acquire the necessary mindset to view a deal from the shoes of the customer and to prepare for appropriate responses (or defenses).

2.3   DIRECT YOUR PITCH TO THE RIGHT PERSON OR PERSONS

Has your organization ever found it challenging anytime to get the picture of who is (are) the right person who would play a dominant role in the buying of your goods or services? Has your sales team been caught wrong-footed in addressing the sales pitch? Are there situations where the customer organization is opaque and the team composition and roles unclear?

We should not sidestep the most obvious, perhaps the most critical and sometimes the most undermined aspect—pitching to the right person. We are not suggesting that salesmen make fundamental errors in reaching out to the right people—certainly not in good companies. The issue revolves around how quickly you are able to target the right persons, what varied approaches you employ with the different persons of the buying team and how you contribute to meshing the process and the people effectively. Further, organizations are often complex, not just in their structure but even more in buying dynamics. In many B2B situations, the buyer is a large team of people, with functional representations from technical, purchasing, finance, IT, HR, marketing, production and supply chain, among others. Some even have sub-functions like design, costing, packaging, quality control, market research and regulatory joining the team.

External parties like consultants may also join the team. It is quite possible that the team is not officially declared to the seller organization and needs to be 'figured' out. The traditional framework of buyers and influencers does not fully capture this complexity. The team may also include many vertical levels—assistant manager, manager, head of the department and vice president, among others and several combinations of them. That is just the structure. The dynamics of how each of these functional representatives gets involved in the process is even more misty and variable. Some of them come in and go out of the process a few times. Some of them change during the long buying-selling process. Some of them don't articulate anything in the presence of the seller but share their comments privately and are therefore difficult to out-guess.

> For example, the salesman for a materials handling system spent three months with the director of western warehouse operations of a large New York-based manufacturing company. All along, this contact assured the salesman that he made all the decisions for his area. Unfortunately, competition got the business for the four *regional* warehouses because it won over the VP of operations in New York, who had the budget approval for all new warehouse systems.[4]

Unilever (and many other global multinationals), one of our large potential customers of fragrances, often had a maze of functions and managers to deal with. Sometimes, it was the marketing that assumed the leadership for a purchase situation ('project brief' or 'brief' as it is usually known) and sometimes it was the technical. The purchasing and finance/commercial were always there but their roles were different in different situations. There were also occasions when the divisional head or the CEO took part in discussions. It was important to map this structure and dynamics for every project with the customer, sometimes, as we went along rather than at the beginning. A project for one of the variants of a product-line under one beauty brand could have about 10–15 managers of Unilever in the frame. It was further complicated by the fact that these managers operated from different geographies and even continents.

---

[4] Benson P. Shapiro and Ronald S. Posner, *Making the major sale* (*Harvard Business Review*, July–August 2006).

Organization Structure and Dynamics

How does one ensure that sales efforts are directed at the right person or the set of persons? 'No correlation exists between the functional area of a manager and his or her power within a company. It is not possible to approach the data-processing department blindly to find decision makers for a new computer system, as many sellers of mainframes have learned. Nor can one simply look to the CEO to find a decision maker for a corporate plane. There is no substitute for working hard to understand the dynamics of the buying company.'[5]

It became an obsession for our team to draw up organizational structures of customers, apparent roles of each individual, possible dynamics of the process and revise it whenever new information came to our knowledge. The more concrete our salesmen got with this information, the more successful they were. Salesmen are sometimes not thorough with this, due to their own lack of understanding, their lack of questioning ability or, simply, their tendency to 'assume' such information. In some cases, you may be able to ask for this information from the customer. In our experience, the 'official' word is only partly reflective of the dynamics and constructing the rest of the jigsaw is the responsibility of the salesman. Care should also be taken to ensure that salesmen do not 'hoard' such information, often limiting its utility to the whole organization.

In addition to the understanding outlined above, it is important, as a second step, to decode individual importance of the managers and, specifically, their veto and influencing (obstructing or supporting) powers. This can be harder as it needs to be sensed, based on clues and random comments. *Selling to the right set of people in customer organizations, even as it sounds obvious, is a diligent practice that needs to be built into the routines of the Account Manager.*

As would be seen in subsequent pages, the different stakeholders in the customer organization have different needs, and therefore, selling to them is not a one-size-fits-all approach.

In family managed companies (Asia and Latin America are full of them), there is a further complexity of fuzzy roles of many directors or managers, many of whom seem to play overlapping roles. Their official titles are not always indicative of their powers or responsibilities. It can be further compounded by the fact that they can appear and 'disappear' during the long engagement keeping the account teams confused as to 'how' much to sell to them.

---

[5] Thomas V. Bonoma, *Major sales: Who really does the buying?* (*Harvard Business Review*, July–August 2006).

If it is your first large project with a company that has a complex organization and fuzzy roles, play safe by keeping multiple contacts informed of the progress, solutions and so on. It would become clearer at some stage as to who matters how much. A further calibration can be done at that stage.

Account managers may make the mistake of leaving out some too early in the game, not being perceptive to the familial equations.

In my association with a broad business intelligence program for the account management teams of a large global corporation, the managers often shared the complexity of their customer organizations, which typically are the top 100 or 200 companies (including state enterprises) in a market. The norm in this corporation is to deal with CIOs who managed technology procurement on behalf of end-user departments and were considered the custodian of technology architecture. However, a deeper engagement could only be achieved as a result of getting across to user teams and meeting their stated and unstated agenda, even while navigating the CIOs and the CFOs (who controlled the wallets). In the same company, there may be different 'buyers' for different projects—for an existing application, the end-user matters more. For a payroll or an HR administration system, the HR head should be the prime partner for conversation. For a new white space opportunity, it could well be the CEO or someone at the C level. This needs to be understood well by all members of the account team.

A simplified case of the healthcare equipment industry is used here as illustration. In this industry, the target buyers in a hospital are the purchasers, department (urology, cardiology, etc.) heads, doctors, lab technicians and, of course, the finance group. If you are in a repeat sale situation of equipment already bought (re-buy) by the same hospital, your main target is the purchaser (and maybe the finance person). If you are selling equipment that is based on a new technology (for that customer), your target maybe the department head, who would want to know how the equipment helps his or her operations. If you are selling a new generation of complete solutions to some of the doctors' problems in post-operative care, doctors become your chief target to convince. If you are selling a newer version of existing equipment that has new operator-friendly features or new electronic gizmos, the technician who operates such machines becomes the key person who would need to evaluate the machine. If your product is still in prototype phase and you are looking for additional technology or usage inputs to making it relevant with the necessary cutting edge, technology group in the hospitals or technology consultants hospitals hire are your prime go-to-people. In this case, your co-creators or collaborators are the real 'buyers' as well. In all these different scenarios, the purchasing is never out of the picture and need concurrent management. Thus, between the same vendor and the same customer, the 'right person' can be dramatically different in different sales situations.

Experienced account managers tend to do these intuitively and this could pose some problems. The practice will disappear when they go, as it is not a documented step in the company's manual. It will fail to detect changes that customers may bring in.

The rules of engagement between vendors and customers change periodically, and account teams must play their roles without ruffling feathers. In a sense, the 'selling' effort is therefore directed at users and direct beneficiaries, even though it may be channeled through several other people. Navigating this delicate ecosystem needs skill and preordained processes.

The most significant advantage of selling to the right person is the saving in time and effort in the pre-sales phase. Engaging with the right person(s) also eases the flow of relevant information transfer from the buyer to the seller. In the pre-sales phase, this is a crucial goal as buyers start to sift through the information and develop short lists of vendors that they would choose from. Account teams will also get to know the buying process as lucidly as possible, at the first stage of discussions. You do not want to be chasing the wrong tail that can derail your momentum. *Imagine that selling is a treasure hunt and you have to cover x number of stops in the fastest time, based on clues and hints. You would definitely not want to waste time at wrong spots (people) or expend your energy (sales efforts) on a circuitous route. Also, it is a race with your competition and thus you need to put your nose ahead somehow. Knowing the right persons and their roles is the key. It should not be forgotten that this is a dynamic chart and may change for every single opportunity.*

I was associated with one glaring case of misstep by one of the leading package software companies, a pioneer in ERPs. Thankfully, I was on the other side. I was a member of the buying team evaluating the best CRM package as part of an overhaul of processes. The company lost the multimillion-dollar order to a specialist supplier who catered (and convinced) better to the user group which I and another colleague represented. The 'big' company was only focused on the IT team and members of the senior management and misread the roles of the members of the large selection team.

For one of your customers, try and gather as much information as possible in the following template—Table 2.1 (you may be surprised that you have missing information even for your longstanding customer). Feel free to add 'more' columns for greater lucidity and articulation:

Table 2.1 Customer contacts mapping

Name	Title	Function	Role in buying	Personality traits relevant	How long in the job	'real' power held	Attitude toward us	Contact strategy suggested
Scott Dell	VP-technology	Technical, R&D, product development	Approve designs, new products, technical recommendations	Moody, talks little, prefers to read documents	12 years	Can veto new products single-handedly	Neutral to positive, lately encouraging	At least once a quarter face-to-face; fortnightly email updates, document updates
Anne Lee	Procurement manager	Purchasing and vendor liaison	Purchasing, vendor interfacing, negotiating, orders and schedules in-charge, vendor evaluation	Cordial but not overtly friendly	4 years, may move in 6 months	Gatekeeper for new vendors or for delisting existing vendors; price decider	Fair	Meet every month; our VP to meet once a quarter; invite for seminars
Kirk Swann	Market innovation manager	New products, new markets, new channels, new promotion	Screens new product ideas and clears from marketing viewpoint	Enthusiastic, less critical but more discerning	5 years, recently promoted to a global role	Can influence new product idea acceptance	Likes us but no favors	Regular, off the normal cycle, bring new ideas

Name of the customer: ABC Corporation
Date of preparation/update: 1 July 2017

Some companies assign star (*) ratings to the contact list, signifying their relative importance. This, however, is not a substitute for an insightful description. Note that title, function and role in buying are not necessarily the same. In large organizations, there could be several R&D managers or procurement managers. Attitude towards your company is likely to be dynamic, although it is somewhat difficult to predicate at the start of the relationship. In some companies, the database of client managers is oversimplified and restricted to birthdays, family details and so on, rather than perceptive information that is highly useful in selling situations and needed for deploying appropriate strategies and tactics.

Some vendors depend on a 'sponsor' among the customer team who could potentially assist in easing the process for a vendor, providing additional information or even swinging decisions. This model, however, has a limited validity as most companies broad-base the large buy decisions and no single person wields as much clout as is sometimes believed.

2.4   SELL TO THE ENTIRE TEAM

Are your sales teams in the habit of practicing active selling with only one (or a few) members of the customer's buying team? Does your account management system mandate and track a comprehensive contact and buy-in program across the full spectrum of the buying teams? Do you sometimes miss out on a business as someone in the buying team did not support your proposal? Are your competitors more successful because they seem to engage with more people?

Just as there is team selling, there is team buying. A good sales team would understand that it takes many people from the customers' side to bless your product or service. They also understand that every action of the customer may or may not be visible to the salesperson and yet can matter. Yet, many times, they are dumbstruck when they discover that a sales opportunity did not materialize as there were objections from some quarters, which became evident too late to address (or were unknown even at the end).

In one of my early visits to Japan, a customer team of eight managers, all in dark blue or black suits, met my team of two people, including me. Our meeting lasted about three hours during which time only two customer representatives spoke. Readers would be familiar with this situation in Japan. After the meeting, I asked my Japanese colleague how the meeting went. My takeout was that it did not go well as most people could not be engaged in a conversation. There is a simple but powerful concept that a good conversation leads to good sales possibilities. My colleague said 'the meeting went well' and I asked him why he said that. He based his comment on three things—one, everyone was taking notes, two, many nodded many times, and three, some spoke and the others spoke among themselves. It was a combination of culture and language barrier that resulted in only two people speaking to us, but all were engaged. In fact, we received correspondences from some of the other managers after the meeting. We were very sensitive to keep everyone on board through the process. It is vitally important to engage all members of the customer team in continuous conversations, even if they are not present in all meetings and even if each one has only a segmental role in buying.

One of the practices we followed when we were selling to large multinationals was to meet the marketing teams and subsequently brief the technical team about the discussions, sometimes on the same day. This ensured that we satisfied everyone's ego, but more importantly, it gave us the opportunity to understand if there are any unraveled issues or perspectives from another functional viewpoint. We had to make sure that we did not become victims of any crossfire in the customer organization and this was our best insurance. It did anger some people on a couple of occasions (only where there are departmental rivalries), but the overall gain outweighed such irritants.

To do this successfully, we always tried to understand the whole team and the profile of the members. Our sales arguments could be tailored to the individual needs when we understood the team dynamics and individual positions better. We also learned it the hard way.

In one instance, we got the opportunity to meet one of the stepbrothers of a business in an Asian market and present our product ideas. We spent a full two hours with this director. The other brother got to know of this and wanted to meet us. We did not quite fathom the internal rivalry at that point. When the other brother met us, he asked us why we did not meet him. (The fact was we did not get an appointment through his secretary and had planned to do it another day.) He was not inclined to listen to our position and blacklisted us. It lasted quite a while! If our account manager had a good understanding that both the directors mattered equally, we could have emerged without a bleeding nose.

In another situation, we presented to the owner-CEO of a large company and were treated enthusiastically, including being hosted a lunch at the directors' lunchroom. Nothing followed, even though the CEO had promised to share the presentation ideas with the team. We then had a meeting with the Head of Business, nearly three months later, and found that the CEO had just casually mentioned about our meeting without suggesting follow-up steps. Our business cards had not been passed on either. You may do one transaction by excluding some relevant people, but you would not have an enduring business. Some of my friends, who had government as their customer, would share with me stories of how one department (or even one desk) would jeopardize important progress made in tenders and deals.

More Contacts, More Sales Opportunities, More Revenue

There is also a positive motivation to sell to the larger group. One of my clients manages the corporate sales function of a large hospitality company in Asia, overseeing the MICE (meetings, incentive travel, conferences and exhibitions) business. Their model of acquiring new businesses includes canvassing the buying team for 'upselling' opportunities after securing the basic contract. Thus, a corporate retreat may start with the vanilla package—meeting room, guest rooms, lunches and dinners—but based on the inputs of actual users and senior management or other department heads in the customer's organization, it often extends to premium cocktails, special entertainment, motivation speeches by eminent speakers, fun games, professional photography, videos, live band, games and so on. The add-ons follow discussions with other stakeholders than the main buyer. These upsold services are many times a significant chunk of the overall contract value and highly profitable, as the basic package is often won through competitive price bidding. This example is applicable to several other industries like banking, software, equipment and packaging industries, where 'add-on' benefits can be attractive to different users. Such bonus is only available through exploiting multiple contacts.

As most B2B transactions involve multiple managers and departments, it is not just important to get that list, but consciously plan contact and communication activities commensurate with their importance, role and seniority. 'An explosion of communication vehicles and interaction channels has ratcheted up the expectations of business purchasers. Many more influencers and decision makers are now involved in the purchasing process, and business buyers too have been shaped by their consumer shopping experience. As a result, their behavior has become more consumer-like. There is no longer such a thing as a simple cold call: customers expect a sales rep to be extremely knowledgeable about their business and perhaps even their own individual profile.'[6]

It should not be left to the whims or comfort of the account manager but embedded into the process. Sales leaders will need to act as role models when they meet customers. As we would discuss later, this strategy is also imperative to ensure that the company's contact strength is not confined to the account manager and his or her buddy on the other side.

Invisible Managers Are Common

What happens if there are invisible players in the buying team—managers who are not seen in meetings or who act behind the scenes with some degree of influence? The only way to 'reach' these people may be through the people that account managers interact with. Thus, the solutions and the story (elaborated in a later chapter) have to be sold to direct contacts, arming them with necessary information to 'sell' further internally to their other colleagues. Knowing the existence of such invisible people and their likely interests is another vital area for account managers to work on.

Account relationships are long-lasting and many team members of the customer will move and take on different responsibilities, as part of their career progression (either in the same company or in another company who could be your potential customer). Practicing a level playing field with thedifferent managers helps immensely in developing goodwill with these managers. You can reap more with one seed. (Equally if you have neglected a buying team member once, you probably will lose his or her patronage forever.)

[6] Oskar Lingqvist, Candace Lun Plotkin and Jennifer Stanley, *Do you really understand how your business customers buy?* (*Mckinsey Quarterly*, February 2015).

2.5   SELL AT ALL LEVELS

Are your salesmen capable of effectively engaging all levels of the customer's organization? Does your company have credibility with senior level managers of your customer? What is the top of the mind recall of your company among the customer's senior management?

One of the corollaries to selling to the whole team is to sell at all levels, vertically. This is crucial, especially if senior management is somehow involved in the decision-making or if your product or service is critical to the success of the customer. Salesmen are sometimes comfortable to transact only at certain levels and cannot move up the hierarchy of the customer. For example, most salesmen would need other senior people to handhold, if they need to meet people at C levels. This is a reflection of their lack of skills, lack of confidence or the company culture. The nature of conversations is different at different levels and few account managers develop the versatility that is required to straddle comfortably. In the B2B sphere, it is common for teams of people to visit customer teams. Using these multiple opportunities, vendors can expose salesmen to different functions and hierarchies. Confidence building measures and conversational training are other important tools to achieve this.

Referring to the principles of selling to CEOs, the *Harvard Business Review* has this to say: 'The buyer has privileges that the seller does not. It's up to you to prepare for the meeting and be ready with examples or case studies that demonstrate your awareness of the customer's business context. And then you must be willing to go with the flow if the customer has other topics in mind. It's about active listening: be better prepared and more granular in your questions.'[7]

Do You Usurp Your Salesman's Right?

We made a few simple rules in our organization that eased the path of 'growing up' for account managers. For example, whenever we met customers as a team, only the account manager would engage in price discussions. We were conscious that if senior managers take over price

[7] Frank V. Cespedes, Jay Galeota and Michael Wong, *Salespeople need a strategy for selling to CEOs* (*Harvard Business Review*, 13 October 2016).

negotiations, customers tend to undervalue the account manager. This is not desirable for his confidence or for his future stature with the customer. Senior team members, if present in price discussions, would act as 'support speakers' or amplify points rather than present proposals or alternatives. This is challenging for some senior managers who like to underscore their presence. It needs a conscious understanding of the tactic and regular practice (and avoidance of hegemony).

The other rule we made was that we would consciously seek appointments with CEOs of our customers, as we wanted to engage them in higher order, future-related discussions. To our luck, we were always successful in securing these meetings, even though our product category may not have ranked that high. I have had the opportunity to meet many country level and regional chairmen and CEOs of companies like Unilever, Colgate, Henkel and more and these meetings were always productive and engaging for both sides. We made sure that the agenda of such meetings was appropriate to the level of people we met. We would always bring interesting information or ideas to bounce with people at such level. The point about homework elaborated elsewhere came in handy. For example, some of our discussions centered around struggling brands of the customer and what our thoughts were to address that. We struck a chord with most CEOs whenever we broached this topic. The cascading effect of such meetings can be very unexpected in a positive sense. We sometimes had other managers called into such meetings by the CEOs to join the discussions. This opened up new opportunities instantly. This skill is not easy to acquire and takes time, but regular exposure and mentoring help.

It is common in the corporate banking sector to engage with CFOs of customers, both as a relationship enhancing exercise and as opportunities to identify latent needs. How is this typically accomplished? Many relationship managers (account managers) cannot do this effectively at that level and need their bosses to lead the way. If the bosses step in too often, the relationship managers are never going to acquire the skills in vertical management of customers. They need to be given the impetus and the encouragement to develop the right agenda and conversational skills to engage CFOs on a regular basis. Companies are sometimes guilty of using 'hierarchy' as a crutch to impede the evolution of account managers. Ironically, smaller vendors seem to embrace this easier, as their teams are small (and may be less experienced) and yet they may need to meet C-level people to canvas for business.

If CEOs are not easy to meet (I guess this is a gripe for most account managers), heads of businesses must be met with some regularity. We also sometimes benefitted from business heads moving up to CEO positions, if we had a rapport with the business heads before.

The typical salesperson is usually comfortable and cozy with meeting a few 'like-minded' or similarly positioned people at the customer's end. This stops to work once people move or when there are other overarching purchase considerations. They need to be taken out of their comfort zone and orientated toward meeting a wider hierarchy of people. Our annual key account plans included 'meeting the CEO' or 'meeting the divisional VP' as an action plan, listed with a timeline. Account plans acted almost as our bible and this ensured respect from all participants. If you are treated as a trusted advisor or if your previous meetings with the top people were productive to them, it could give you some tailwinds in getting appointments. It is nevertheless useful to understand the CEO, his or her favorite 'themes' and follow recent speeches. For example, some CEOs keep a strong innovation agenda, some are obsessed with growth, some pursue sustainability, some others speak brand language, some fancy process simplification, some like to focus incessantly on consumer experience and so on. Tailoring the meeting toward such specific interests, while presenting proposals for your products or service, helps. It is important, though, to understand that CEOs are not 'buyers' and account teams cannot expect buying decisions from them. Therefore, hard-sell pitches are out of place and discussions should only be exploratory and idea-germinating sessions. The CEOs play some role (big or small will depend on the company) to keep your company in the frame, give you opportunities or ease your engagement process.

Junior Level Employees Also Matter

The inverse hierarchy mindset is also important. It is many times useful to meet the lower grade officers in the customer hierarchy. This requires some skill and attitude as well. They are usually ignored by their own organizations and are always seeking some identity and recognition. Thanking them for their small acts of support (even making photocopies for you or processing your payment), enquiring about their well-being or even briefing them about discussions with their superiors (if no confidentiality is breached) are useful ways to engage them. Salesmen seldom keep aside time for this as they undervalue the benefits. We have derived many benefits from our interactions at the junior level.

One of our small but growing customers had a limited technical and product development *department in a small town. Fragrance salespersons never visited this department. During one of our meetings with the chemist, our discussion went into their formulation and ingredients used. The chemist then asked us if we could help her with sourcing some special ingredients for some new products, as no supplier was willing to give her samples free of cost. We arranged these materials quickly and earned substantial goodwill with what turned out to be one of the key influencers. We also arranged to include her on our mailing list for scientific and formulary information. We may not able to put a finger on how it helped our business to grow, but I am sure when the vote was tight, the chemist weighed in our favor.*

It is a common practice in Asia to offer personal gifts or invite to dinners people at the lower level of hierarchy. We, however, stayed away from this practice but looked for ways to help them advance professionally and earn their superior's recognition. If we can help a customer's manager achieve his or her objectives, we can expect gratitude in indirect ways and for a long time. Many of these junior staff or managers rise up in the organization to occupy positions of authority. The career rise span has shrunk in recent times as many CEOs and business heads reach those positions by the time they are 40. The brand manager of one of our very successful customers, with whom we began a relationship while dealing with their core brand, became the chief executive of the division (annual turnover $200+ million) in less than 15 years! His company and his team maintained a strong business relationship with our company for most of these years. It had been a highly worthwhile investment.

Construct a table of your top 50 or 100 or 200 customers and write down how many times you have met the CEO (or a person at the very top) in the past 12–18 months. It would tell you how well you are doing on this front and what new actions you need.

2.6   DON'T OFFER SOLUTIONS TOO EARLY

In your sales process, at what stage does your account team offer solutions to customers' problems? Is there a structured form of ascertaining and clarifying customer needs before possible solutions are discussed? Is the structured 'need assessment' step followed as a standard practice and documented?

This is one area where account management differs distinctly from a simple transactional selling situation. A typical salesman is normally well prepared with a standard sales pitch (and perhaps a story) and is usually eager to deliver it early. In B2C or insurance sales type of situations, this practice is common due to two facts—short interactive time and pre-categorization of the customer or consumer based on presumed needs. This may be practiced with both walk-in new customers and repeat buyers.

'The better the job a salesperson or a sales team does in understanding the client's situation, the better relationships they make, the better recommendations they make, the less resistance they encounter and the more deals they close. It's all about the client and the best way to stand out is to know more about them than anyone else.'[8] If the recommendations have to follow the understanding, it is clear that the sequence has to change.

In the B2B world, the fundamentals create this difference. The engagement is a long process and not just one meeting. Each customer's need may be different in several aspects. An automotive tire company trying to sell to Ford, Chrysler, Toyota or Hyundai will face vastly different buying mechanisms, product specifics, performance needs and reasoning. Further, the buying considerations are complex and therefore there are multiple conversations. A good sequence of interactive communication would consist of a series of questions and responses that lead to identification and confirmation of the problem(s) in hand. This is to be followed by a presentation of the solution, logically derived from the articulated problem. Early offer of this, therefore, can at best be based on guesses, which may sometimes be poor judgments. Customers will also resent such an approach as generic rather than tailored.

Conventional salesmen may find it challenging to make the transition (one of the reasons why we were reluctant to hire B2C or retail salespersons for account management). Our account managers were trained to hone the art of asking the right questions.

Questioning to Understand Problems

Questioning is an underrated skill. Many people think and do it their natural way. The problem lies in two things—a preset sequence that does not borrow from responses to the questions and too many close-ended questions,

---

[8] Eric Baron, *Innovative Team Selling* (Wiley, May 2013).

too early in the conversation. If you ask yes or no questions too early, you get just that answer and no elaboration. It is the elaboration in customer's own words that is a good feed for your further questions or for identifying needs. This premise is very simple, and yet, the majority of account managers are either poor questioners or poor listeners or both. This is a sure formula for poor meeting outcomes. Imagine that you need to visit a doctor and the doctor asks you a series of preset questions and does not take leads from your responses. What treatment advice or medication should you then expect? Would it cure your illness?

We must encourage pre-analysis of the customer's problems, yet it pays to logically bring it out during conversation with the customer. Thus, even if you have thought of a potential solution, it would be more convincing if it is offered after an agreement is reached on the problem. It helps the customer to accept it as the tailored 'remedy' to his illness, rather than a panacea dished out to everyone. It is even better if you can get the customer to articulate your solution in a logical sequence of questions and answers. You got your buy-in straightaway. Customers also rate vendors who can curate solutions from problem analysis much better than 'straitjacket' salesmen.

In one of my coaching assignments for a large technology company, account managers were asked to identify four or five key strategic issues for a chosen customer and then offer solutions to tackle each of them. These were experienced account managers, about to step into leadership roles in their organization. Yet, they would agonize over the sequence and would often put the cart before the horse. Many of them would project the solution as an issue or derive the issue from the solution they have already conjured in their minds. In some cases, problems were stated as 'leveraging national distribution network'—which, in fact, is the solution to the problem of 'stagnating sales'. In other words, it is easier to think of solutions in isolation rather than derive it from a good analysis of the problem and there lies the malaise.

Solutions to Real or Presumed Problems?

Salesmen may also assume a lot of things when they are obsessed with advocating their preconceived solution. In many B2B situations, salesmen, for instance, may assume that reducing cost is an important criterion when the real issue could be reliability or flexibility or performance or scalability. The account manager's mission is not to sell a product or service but solve a customer's problem that the customer articulates or concurs with. This is captured in Fig. 2.1.

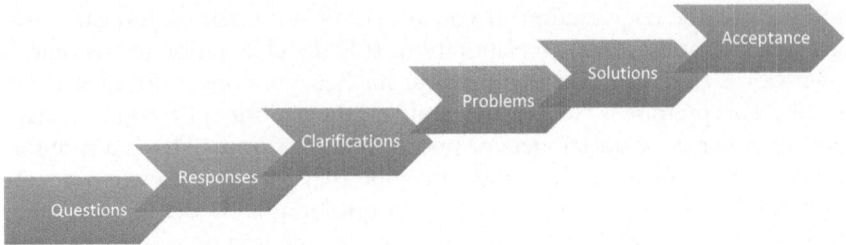

Fig. 2.1 Need and solution sequence

Our annual training included role-plays to get this sequence right and build it in as a habit. Our trainers would repeatedly drive home the concept of 'funneling' wherein questions are asked in a certain sequence so that you can distill the responses and narrow the outcome, from a broad range of general responses. This question-problem-solution method may take a bit longer but is a more certain way of matching solutions to the problems as identified by the customer. As products or services could be complex, this method also helped both the customer and our company in clarifying the problem or the opportunity and its sub-elements in greater detail. If you sold a wrong product or service, it would come to haunt you, as the customer would direct the blame squarely at you. We were also successful in getting customers to rewrite their briefs in some instances, as a result of this dialogue as more clarity emerged from the discussions.

Over time, it is possible to identify broad strands of needs and for each strand, develop a solution matrix or building blocks. This is a good way to approach product/solution development. However, in the eyes of the customer, solutions should always be seen as logical responses to need assessment rather than pre-conceived.

One way to standardize the questioning is to develop a checklist. It should be used only as a guide and not as a 'questionnaire' that takes away the benefits of a two-way interaction. Questioning and avoidance of the assumption 'rush' is also covered in a later chapter.

The next time you visit a customer who has a new opportunity, try to spend the first 10 or 15 minutes asking just questions and jotting responses. (It can be difficult for conventional salesmen.) There are even theories that postulate that in sales conversations, you must speak only one-third of the time and cede the rest of the time to the customer. The practice will help account managers see the patterns in responses, synthesize the issues and summarize a well-articulated set of problems. A revered marketing professor at my alma mater would often say, 'our role as market researchers is not to find the answers for our clients, but to help them ask the right questions.' That is the power of good questioning.

2.7   PLAN METICULOUSLY FOR JOINT CUSTOMER VISITS

How well are visits by a team of people from your side synchronized? How do you leverage the group dynamics in order to secure maximum advantage with the customers? What is the scope and depth of training and preparation for joint visits?

It is common for a team of people to meet customers in the B2B context. The aim of the group visits is usually to offer a spectrum of functional expertise and complement the coordinating player (typically the account manager). Our teams very often would consist of an account manager, a supervisor, a product selection expert, maybe a marketing or a market research person and in some situations, the country head or a VP. The way the team presented itself as a seamless group of experts and the manner in which the customers perceived the overall team effort was something we deeply cared for. We followed a few simple rules.

Roles of Team Members

For a start, no person who did not have a role in a meeting would join a meeting. In some exceptional cases, a new manager or a young trainee would join as an observer as part of his or her on-the-job training. If the managers on the other side were new, we would do a formal introduction of the team along with our roles in the organization. The role-play would generally be decided before the meeting. We appointed one of the members of the team as the 'champion' or the 'lead speaker' and the others would rally around him or her. The choice of the champion depended on circumstances and the agenda of the meeting. It was usually the account manager or the immediate supervisor as they had direct client responsibilities. We were keen that in the customer's eyes the account managers and the account team resided as the mainstay of the relationship. If the agenda included sharing of new marketing ideas or market research findings, the appropriate person would take the lead. The role of the senior team member or the VP was to bring discussions to some closure and sometimes to share global trends, company activities and so on. The country head or the VP would also play his or her role in helping remove knots and extricate the team from difficult situations.

In typical B2B customer meetings, the roles are usually clear but the conversation dynamics and the interplay are not. Players jump in when it's not necessary and can sometimes contradict their colleagues. Even if many of the participants are familiar with the agenda of the day, there must be a mechanism to restrain their enthusiasm to talk out of turn or to monopolize the conversation. The meeting is like a train on tracks. The track adherence has to be preplanned and executed well.

The Conductor of an Orchestra

In my former company context, most of the opening approaches and the script for a meeting were prepared before the meeting so that it was synchronized and flowed smoothly. The best analogy is that of a musical performance where there is a conductor and many individual instrumentalists. The whole orchestra blends in seamlessly and even if the music is rehearsed, it achieves its objective of pleasing the audience in a creative way. Account managers were trained to be the orchestra conductor and many times did only that. There is sometimes a misplaced opinion that the account manager is the Hercules and he plays all instruments. While he may have the capability, it is not always necessary to do that.

In one of my global assignments, a 'loner' account manager reported to me. He considered himself as the jack-of-all-trades and would normally not allow anyone to visit his customers. That he was a successful salesman made it difficult for many people to attempt to mend his ways. I had to spend long hours, use persuasion and mild orders to convince him to carry other managers in his team. He started with functions like market research where his familiarity was low and expanded gradually to other managers. Companies will need to take a call on the concept of lone rangers and groom account managers to effectively function as the conductor. And yet, they must have adequate familiarity in the different areas and should not be a glorified escort.

Organizational Goals Are Paramount

In a team-selling context, the goals of the organization take precedence over individual or departmental objectives. Thus, there may be situations involving giving up of something to achieve something bigger or a minor role for a key manager. The best cellist of a famous orchestra may have very little to play in a particular symphony.

One of world's top three customers in the business of beauty and homecare business paid the best compliment for our approach. When asked to recommend a good account manager from our competitors or from other partners like advertising agencies and packaging suppliers (as we were looking to expand our team), the vice president-commercial of this company said that there wasn't anyone as good as our person responsible for the account at that time. His remarks were as much a testimony of the individual's own capabilities as her ability to effectively rally the team around her. That account manager is now a successful top executive in the same company, working in the North American operations.

Keep Some Constancy

One other key consideration in joint visits is the constancy of the core members of the team. How would you respond if one of your vendors presented 15 different people at three consecutive meetings, with just one manager as a common participant? It is mind-boggling to keep track of the different people and their roles, especially if their participation in the meetings were fleeting. Things can get complicated further for a customer if you consider that they meet many vendors of many products and services in a cycle. It pays to keep the core the same, at least during the course of a project or an opportunity. Large organizations with multiple departments and layers are often guilty of not paying attention to this aspect. Smaller organizations, on the other hand, have an advantage by default. In my former fragrance team, we kept the majority of the people constant with each customer. As the sales cycle involved multiple steps and meetings, this ensured that most of the participants knew the full story of the opportunity like the back of their palms. When you make this call consciously, you will start to question the role of each person being picked to join a visit, instead of pretending to 'play safe' by picking more than appropriate people. Inclusion in delegations to meet customers should never be deemed as a reward ticket to a special show.

When you visit a large customer next time with a group of managers, identify their individual roles in the meeting, plan the script and interventions and rehearse it to the maximum extent you can. This should include who will take what type of questions and who is authorized to make commitments. Where permitted, you can record such meetings with customers for playback and analysis. A lot of awkwardness while meeting customers can be avoided by these steps.

2.8   CONDUCT HONEST ANALYSES OF FAILURES

What is the norm for reviewing and analyzing failed projects or attempts in your organization? Do your account managers feel secure to report and analyze the full facts concerning failures? Is there a culture of deep introspection and learning from such experiences, without a fear of witch-hunt? Do you practice a corrective process based on the findings?

Not all attempts will yield a positive result. In B2B transactions, this could happen after a lot of toil and after resources have been deployed for months or years. It is therefore imperative and fair to do a thorough introspection of what went right or what went wrong in a 'lost' transaction. Both loss of existing businesses and loss of a potential order will qualify for this. Companies possibly do one or the other and may do it cursorily. It would be easy to put the blame on one event or one person in the whole chain and console oneself that the loss was not due to lack of best efforts. That would rob us the opportunity of learning from the failed effort. The learning can potentially impact your current processes, your current teams, your current rules and regulations or your current abilities to execute your intentions. Far from just being a verdict on a person, this may force more fundamental changes to your account management strategies and practice.

The analysis can be time-consuming and may open up a can of worms, much to the discomfiture of managers in the selling organization. In our company, the analysis was made a routine. The account managers would lead the information collection, insights and analysis of possible reasons for the failure. They were encouraged to be frank as the essential purpose was to learn appropriate lessons for the next outing. During the annual sales conference, account managers would present one case of success and one case of loss or failure, for the benefit of all account managers. Our success ratio on projects was about 25–30% of the pipeline and therefore it was acceptable that account managers would lose some opportunities. There were invaluable lessons to learn from these analyses, more than any external case study or training programs could serve.

Staying Objective to Learn the Right Lessons

The objectivity of the analysis was scrupulously maintained. Over time, we categorized the 'loss' reasons into five or six major heads and a few sub-heads. Some of the insights were telling, especially when the reasons repeated themselves with regularity. Poor understanding of customer needs (wrong starts), inadequate chasing during critical stages of the project (dozing off on the account), mishandling of objections, communication slips, complacency, lack of understanding of people roles or dynamics, lack of good orchestration across different stakeholders, poor closing were some common characteristics. There were very few instances when our solutions were objectively inferior. Some salesmen showed profoundly troubling tendencies in one or more of these, making the habit hard to kick. Surprisingly, there were very few losses due to pricing issues. Our pricing judgment was generally right. Such positive reinforcements also help in building confidence among the team for future transactions.

One aspect that came to the fore was that in many cases, it was difficult to ascribe the loss to a single reason. While that is to be expected, account managers would candidly admit that the project did not go our way as our relationship vis-à-vis the customer suffered a decline, which was not noticed in time even when a competitor was gaining ground. As we argue in other paragraphs, in a long relationship, grounds for apathy are plenty and could lead to adverse results if not noticed and corrected.

In one instance, we lost a potential business simply because we could not commit to a fast delivery of the first order as the customer was racing to change to a new fragrance. This would happen if two potential fragrances finished on par during the evaluation and a competitor is able to fast-track delivery. We learned our lesson and from then on built a better buffer of common raw materials so that we could meet such exigencies. Sometimes customers delay their decisions and shift the consequences to the supplier. This was one such case.

If you can desist from the blame game, many practical lessons can be learned from analysis of failures. This is the fundamental principle of 'postmortem' in the medical domain. The outcome cannot be reversed but the recurrence could be avoided. The US army conducts an AAR. (after action review) in order to precisely gauge what went right and what went wrong. In military operations, you cannot afford to make mistakes once, let alone again. Even in major sporting encounters, team managements analyze reasons for win or loss as learnings could be quickly applied to upcoming games in a long season. The devil is always in the details and thus digging deeper into the causes, however irritable the process may be, will serve the purpose better.

Professor Birkinshaw of London Business School recommends drawing up a balance sheet to assess a project's return on failure. 'On one side, consider your 'assets'. These might include: What have you learned about your customers' needs and preferences? Do you need to change any of your assumptions? What insights have you gained into future trends? What have you discovered about how you work as a team? On the other side, look at your 'liabilities': costs, both financial and less tangible costs such as damage to reputation or morale. Bottom line: What are the key insights and takeaways for your business?'[9]

The Customer Can Help You

We also always tried to ask the customer for the reason for our loss. Contrary to skeptics, we did get to hear the official version on many occasions and on reflection were able to corroborate such reasons. If this dialogue can be conducted honestly, it is a sign of matured supplier-customer relationship. Like all other salesmen's habits, this is something they shirk, if there is no systemic expectation of a postmortem.

Analyze all your lost opportunities in the past 12 months, by account manager and by reason. (To start with, you could analyze the losses arising from your top customers who account for 60–70% of your sales.) Examine the mode data (high-frequency reason or account manager) and then construct the possible explanations. It would cover a vast gamut from people to processes to judgments to speed. These explanations should then lead to a corrective action plan for future opportunities. As you mature in this process, seek out customers' assessment of the reasons as well to further corroborate your findings. Customers also tend to respect vendors with a learning culture more.

---

[9] Professors J. Birkinshaw and Kathy Brewis, *How to fail successfully* (London Business School, 28 November 2016).

2.9   DEVELOP RESILIENCE TO HANDLE PRICE ARGUMENTS

What is the role of pricing in buy decisions for your products or services? Are your account managers trained to handle price objections and defend your pricing? Do you foster a culture of price and profitability awareness with the account teams? Does your account team feel safe, informed and comfortable in engaging customers in successful price discussions?

The concept and importance of pricing in B2B are often reduced to thinking of 'negotiation' where vendors give up some room and buyers do a similar thing. Pricing is a more nuanced tool and needs the same amount of matured understanding as other aspects of account management. Price may be a very important component of B2B sales transactions (though not always the main one), especially in view of the possible size and repetitiveness of the business. We need to discuss the psychological basis for you and your account managers to achieve a result that is favorable to you. It is one of the hardest conundrums for salesmen. When confronted with a customer comment that competitors offer lower prices, salesmen can get stumped as they quickly deem this comment to be a deal breaker and feel stressed about it. That is the intention of the purchaser—that you buckle in. Matured salesmen can handle this as they follow a systematic way of verifying the claim and offering counterarguments. They can also successfully build the 'value ladder'—loading your unique value propositions—that will justify the higher pricing that you may seek. But managing the price issue should be a well-crafted organizational practice.

It is important to verify the customer's claim, as this could be just a purchase ploy. In Asian conditions, it is more difficult to do this, as customers may not share evidences. Apart from a direct question, the answer could be generated through a series of indirect questions, especially while posing questions to make sure that apples are compared with apples and the timeframe is similar. Purchases during different price periods or products based on different technologies or for different supply quantities will obviously be on different pricing basis.

Winning Your Price

We need to think beyond the negotiation script. Companies design standardized scripts to tackle price negotiation attempts. However, account managers need to be trained to develop comfort with using these scripts as well as to face other unanticipated questions. It is not the focus here to discuss negotiation techniques and approaches, which are available aplenty in literature, but it is important to dwell on the psychology and preparedness of account managers to win a price argument.

The first area is the price culture. Does the account team accept the idea that your products or services can cost more to customers and yet can be justified? Our team was encouraged to carry the conviction that price differences could be due to intrinsic product or service differences and hence our prices may be higher (and should be so if we believe in our superior product or service). In fact, this message was important to not let in the 'commodity mindset'.

The concepts of 'value pricing' and 'customer value' are relevant here. Value pricing is the method by which you first create perceived and real value for your customer and go on to exploit it in pricing. '[V]alue needs to be defined properly. Customers do not buy solely on low price. They buy according to *customer value*, that is, the difference between the benefits a company gives customers and the price it charges. More precisely, customer value equals *customer-perceived* benefits minus *customer-perceived* price. So, the higher the perceived benefit and/or the lower the price of a product, the higher the customer value and the greater the likelihood that customers will choose that product.'[10]

We dissuaded customers from the thought that two fragrances for a particular brand or application have to cost the same. Customers usually knew they did not, but would still try to engage in negotiations, as fragrances formed a significant percentage of the product cost, for most categories.

Pricing Ideas for B2B

One of the tactics mentioned by expert negotiators is to get a quid pro quo if indeed you need to concede some discount. This could be in the form of higher order quantity, higher lot quantity, faster payments (even

[10] Ralf Leszinski and Michael V. Marn, *Setting value, not price* (*McKinsey Quarterly*, February 1997).

advance payments), longer tenure of the business, built-in price increase after x months and so on. The last concept is interesting.

It is a normal convention that when order quantities increase, customers demand better prices (economic principle). However, one of the top multinational customers offered us a 'reverse price model' whereby the price would go up as quantities increased. The logic is based on the fact that when quantities increase, it meant that the customer's product was successful in the market and this was a way of sharing their fortunes (and the risks in the launch phase). It also meant that we were indirectly asked to fork out a subsidy for introduction of a new product. This concept was applied in one instance but could be a useful approach if the demand pattern is unpredictable at the beginning of a new business or product. This may have relevance in situations involving new product launches or innovative/disruptive introductions. Agreeing to share the risk (and the reward) is a good way of fortifying stakeholdership. Thus, account teams need to be geared up to innovate price plans if the situation demands. This is more than mere sharing of the price gap at the start of a negotiation.

The other relevant concept in B2B is to balance the basket pricing rather than a rigid transaction level approach. Going by the principle of selling more to an existing customer and seeking a higher share of the wallet, we shifted our approach to monitor profitability at customer level rather than at product level, as we sold several fragrances to a customer for their many brands. You win some and lose some. We are not really referring to a 'loss' here but developing comfort with varying product profitability. This also implies that pricing is customer dependent and that is how it should be. A large existing customer thus enjoys special pricing intrinsically by this approach, not just due to potential quantities but from the nature and quality of relationship. Accountants will resist this idea, as their pricing concept hinges purely on product or service cost. The concept of 'special' pricing enjoyed by top customers is similar to the loyalty scheme applied in a variety of consumer industries.

Empowering the Account Managers

Account managers like to enjoy some pricing freedom. While ceding this, we need to make sure that they are trained to use it prudently and to seek approval when it is appropriate. If it does not break your back, it may be useful to let the account managers experiment their skills a bit, even make small mistakes in the bargain. If an account manager shows a pattern of repeating mistakes (of bigger magnitudes), we would then need a discussion. These measures are part of empowering the account managers to be self-sufficient in price discussions and to overcome fear of such prospects. This move is also important to ensure that the account manager owns the pricing decision and fully understands its implications to the company rather than merely following orders. An ideal account manager would act like an owner and even offer suggestions to the company to improve pricing and profitability.

Very often, companies tend to apply the insurance model of pricing, which is fixed and is not conducive to relationship-based pricing approach. When you need to go back to a customer for price increase arising out of cost increases, the account teams' ownership aspect will help. All these arguments can be slightly different if your product is a commodity and customer's purchase decision is based purely on prices. Even then, it will be useful to establish some differences in service or in other terms that can contribute to a small price premium. In the IT hardware industry this is quite common, for example, in products like switches, firewalls, backup storage and so on. How to position your company for premium pricing in a commodity industry is a topic by itself. It is one of the fundamental concepts in services marketing.

Some salesmen would buckle quickly and offer discounts or a referral to the senior management when challenged on price. That would be a clear sign of organizational weakness and would be exploited by the buyer every time.

One of my early training opportunities I had was when I visited a top customer with my boss, a swashbuckling confident Australian, Nick Hagop. After product discussions, the customer remarked, 'your price is high, though'. Nick's reply was 'maybe'. He paused to see if the customer added any follow-up comment or needed a further response. Nothing came and we carried on with the rest of the conversation and the price issue never came up again. Nick had perfected a first response (and probably a second response if the issue persisted) strategy in such situations and that was to blunt the argument offensively. This approach worked due to a combination of understanding customer's position and having the skills to face challenging buying tactics. Extensive and repeated training and role-plays help in honing such skills and attitude among account managers. In industries where pricing is on a continuum (due to several varying factors), a high degree of skill in conducting price discussions backed by a good organizational strategy is essential.

When you draw up your next training schedule for account teams, include a discussion on what should be the tenor and approach your company should adopt with top customers in pricing matters. This should include opinions on aggressive pricing, defense strategies, justification approach and so on. Develop an inventory of 'price arguments' that your customers advance from time to time so that each one could be worked on. Role plays that bring in customer viewpoints and arguments will enhance the utility of such an exercise. Besides generating an inventory of approaches, this would also ensure that account teams are sensitized to your company's performance expectations on the 'pricing' parameter.

CHAPTER 3

Strategies for Deep Customer Engagement

3.1   IDENTIFY THE THREAD TO YOUR CUSTOMER'S STRATEGY

Do you make diligent efforts to understand or follow the customer's overall goals and strategies where your product or service has a role? Are your sales teams equipped with the knowledge to engage customers in strategy (customer's) discussions? Does your sales team have the skills to relate to customer's strategies and align your products or services accordingly? Do you sometimes find that competitors seem to offer solutions that more closely mirror the strategic needs of the customers? Are you able to offer solutions in anticipation of the customer's articulation of his problems?

Most salesmen know a customer's history. A good lot will read their 'present' well. Only a few seek to understand and decode the customer's future. Over the last few years, I have been associated with coaching sales teams of an iconic global technology and consulting company. The sales teams are required to do an individual project covering a key customer of theirs, and present in very few pages, the customer's strategic strengths and weaknesses vis-à-vis the industry and key competitors, and propose recommendations to address them. This is not a pitch for products or services but a high-level strategic insight exercise. For many sales participants

© The Author(s) 2018   53
B. Shankar, *Nuanced Account Management*,
https://doi.org/10.1007/978-981-10-8363-1_3

in the program, this is a struggle. Their natural ocular is only the 'pain' points of the contact they have (CXO or CIO or just operating managers) or the ones that are articulated by the customer. Thus customers are in active or passive mode depending on whether needs have been articulated or not. In their approach, the trigger is with the customer, and more specifically, the salesperson's chief contact. Their strategic thoughts center around IT applications and solutions and nothing beyond. This is a classic behavior of salesmen who have had traditional grooming in product-push environments. They imagine a screen before them that does not allow them to see the more fundamental issues challenging the customer. In some cases, they contribute to erecting that screen. The companies may also not have a culture of embedding strategic analyses as part of account management tasks.

'From the customer's point of view, the greatest need for improvement is in salespeople's knowledge of the customer's business and industry (39% of customers expressed dissatisfaction in this area).'[1] The authors studied 120 sales leaders and 200 customers in a variety of industries to reach this conclusion.

Strategy is now a commonly used tool, even in the everyday realm: High school students strategize their exam preparations; train commuters plot a strategy to reach their workplace quickly and efficiently; homemakers have a strategy to balance their budgets and so on. So why is strategy not part of the daily language of account managers? A strategic analysis of the customer, which includes a deep understanding of his value chain and the customer's own advantages and disadvantages vis-à-vis his key peers, helps in going beyond what is immediately visible and what is known to operating managers at the customer's end. It captures the CEO perspective that would be useful in many ways, least of all to anticipate what is coming. It is also beneficial in engaging the customer in a positive dialogue on the 'future' contours of the customer's business and gaining valuable insights as well as earning credibility with the customer. A strategy dialogue with customers also helps a vendor enhance their point of difference versus the peers. This has the potential to set the account manager apart from other vendors serving the same customer.

It takes some effort and a lot of coaching to get a conventional account manager to take a step back and look at clients strategically, in their own

---

[1] Philip Kreindler and Gopal Rajguru, *What B2B customers really expect* (*Harvard Business Review*, April 2006).

marketspace. A good account manager knows not just his industry well but is also an authority on the industry of the customer. It can be a tall order but is rendered easier by the fact that in many companies where account management is practiced well, a manager is accountable for only a few customers at any point of time.

One of our customers started off well with a small range of products and by clever pricing, packaging and product essentials had captured a decent market share in the markets they entered (against entrenched multinational brands). That was just the first step. The small company, with limited strategic thinking capabilities (just the dynamic young promoter), had to think beyond these primitive steps, as their confidence was high. We engaged the customer in a deeper strategic analysis that included market opportunity analysis, product portfolio and possible extensions, customer segmentation, product upgrades, distribution imperatives and so on. We were not strategy consultants but just an ingredient supplier and did not charge for the strategy services. The resultant strategy was still the customer's own construct, but we added valuable insights into it and were considered a higher order supplier, giving us important competitive advantage. We served the company prolifically for the next 15 years, often meeting 80% of their requirements as the customer galloped at scorching rates of over 25% annual growth by expanding into new segments and new product categories. The customer remained open to C-level consultations on a regular basis. After I moved on to my own consulting, we discussed possibilities of my assistance in helping the customer expand to other Southeast Asian markets.

Training to Think Strategically

The essential requirement for a culture of 'strategic thinking' was training the account management team to do strategic homework for the customer, map their competitive position, identify strengths and weaknesses, make reasonable predictions of customer's possible goals (and get it confirmed later) and have the confidence to engage in such a conversation. As a part of this education, different strategic frameworks like SWOT (strengths, weaknesses, opportunities and threats) analysis, Porter's five forces analysis of the industry, PEST analysis and so on were introduced with an application focus. It was not enough if the SWOT analysis or the PEST analysis for a customer was done. Account managers had to draw up business and commercial implications from each of the insight identified.

For example, if the threat to our customer is 'new nimble competition', the implications are novel products, quicker go-to-market efforts, innovative pricing, guerilla marketing tactics, regular introduction and rationalization of new products, flexible manufacturing set up and so on. One word in the analysis could thus have several implications. Companies who do such analyses do them perfunctorily without extracting the deeper insights.

To achieve an effective level of the strategic understanding, both the account team and vendor organization have to invest in time, money and other resources. Customers will not be swayed by surface level knowledge or analysis. This is a prerequisite to aiming for a large share of the customer's wallet and to instigate proactive work. It is also a precondition to being considered an advisor. The payoff will come in the form of long-term loyalty of customers.

When engaging customers in strategic discussions (concerning their strategies), the difficult part is to tell the customer frankly their faults and missteps. Our sales team was also trained in appropriate vocabulary to articulate such things. The fact that most of the sales team had a management degree did make things easier in India, but that did not quite stop us from deploying the initiative to other markets in Southeast Asia, where the default qualification was a bachelor's degree. It is possible that some salesmen have strong analytical capabilities while the others depend on intuition. Training programs could be tailored according to the natural styles.

Some salespersons may argue that not every customer is interested in this discussion and may sometimes be coy about sharing strategic information. While this could be somewhat true, it is still useful to approach customers for a general conversation that could lead to a strategic discussion of their priorities. We were never rebuffed on this initiative, even in countries like Japan where frank and open discussions happen gradually, if at all. If your company believes in rewriting the engagement rules, this could be one starting point. Customers' initial reservation often stems from industry practices rather than their own skepticism when you are the first vendor to take to strategy conversations.

The strategic dialogue also helped us in other ways. Based on early indication on new initiatives and priorities that we gained from such discussions, we initiated 'internal' readiness projects. In the fragrance industry, the supplier gets about 1–2 months to submit product options against a formal customer brief. If you want sure shot success, it needs 6–12 months, including relevant market research, trial and error and others.

Anticipating projects that are likely to come in gave us valuable time to get battle ready for a project. Our success rate in such predicted projects was obviously much higher. It could even lead to a situation that effectively blocks competitive moves. I am sure our competitors had similar ideas as well, but our dogged pursuit of this approach and the strong execution perhaps was the difference. It may be simpler for companies to start off with a standard template for the customer strategy document and refine it further in due course, as familiarity builds up. The important thing is not to stop with known facts. Intelligent visualization of additional facts and deriving unique competitive insights are more critical.

Given the fact that most large companies will definitely have a three or five or even ten-year horizon for their strategic plans, it would be ideal to do a multi-year strategy exercise. Reliance Industries, a large conglomerate in India, recently launched their 4G telecom services. The foundation for the IT architecture and services began three years ago and large IT players vied with each other to develop their own strategic insights as part of the bidding process. Thus, in many situations, the strategy exercise can become an important competitive tool at the bidding stage itself.

Essentials of the Strategic Analysis

The customer strategy analysis would typically consist of the following aspects constructed in a logical flow:

- *Customer's industry analysis and outlook (over the horizon that is considered appropriate)*
- *Product-market landscape of the customer (including market positions, shares)*
- *Segments that customer operates in*
- *Main elements of consumer behavior in these segments*
- *Key current goals (reasonable assumptions or customer's information)*
- *Key current strategies (premium product, price skimming, benefits spectrum offered, distribution channels, promotion methods, product positioning vis-à-vis competitors, etc.)*
- *Advantages enjoyed by the customer (branding, technology, financial, people, channels, etc.)*
- *Disadvantages suffered by the customer vis-à-vis peers*
- *Likely future goals and strategies (this will reflect your understanding of the customer's situation)*

- *Constraints/threats for executing new strategies*
- *Resources required for implementing new strategies*
- *Alternative strategies (Plan B)*
- *Key outcomes (market share, revenue, profitability, etc.) expected and timelines*
- *Action steps to implement new strategies chosen*

At a more sophisticated level, it can include positioning analysis vis-à-vis peers (appropriate charts or quadrant diagrams can be used), value chain analysis, critical success factors in the industry, the client's rating on these factors and so on. In multi-business companies, it would be necessary to do the strategic analysis at business levels as competitive scenarios are likely to be different. The industry scenario for petrol/diesel and lubricants are entirely different for companies like Shell, BP, for example.

Create the CEO's Agenda
Another approach I recommend to account managers is to create the 'CEO's agenda' (this is the customer's CEO). Based on published information, company facts, speeches of the CEO or other senior personnel, commentaries, presentations, press announcements, analyst reports or your interactions, try to construct the CEO's agenda consisting of five or six essential 'to-do' priorities (or things they want to be measured against). You may not have all the data required to do this, but your deep understanding of the customer and his industry should help you in making reasonable assumptions. From this broad agenda, break it down to some specific aspects that could have a bearing on your prospects with the customer. The advantage of this exercise is that you are forcing yourself to assemble a jigsaw puzzle (the CEO's agenda) based on known facts and intelligent inferences. This is the real world of planning. Taking the CEO's perspective leads you to think like the customer —a helicopter view. As a training exercise, get your account managers to do this for some well-known companies like Microsoft, McDonald's and Boeing and compare with the agenda the CEO may have declared (and available in the public domain).

Power and automation technologies leader ABB's CEO Ulrich Spiesshofer announced in 2014,[2] 'We are shifting our center of gravity towards higher growth segments while enhancing competitiveness and lowering risk particularly in our Power Systems division. We are increasing the customer focus of our organization by streamlining it for greater agility and speed. We will drive change with focused 1,000 day programs to

[2] www.abb.com, October 2017.

ensure a successful implementation'. What are the key takeaways for your company if you are a technology vendor to ABB (for instance)? How would that impact your understanding of the opportunities that you envision for your company? If you are a current vendor, what changes and implications does this declaration suggest in your business prospects, priorities or approaches?

3.2   Do Your Homework About the Customer

What is the process followed by your account team in preparation for a target opportunity? How do you ensure that the practice is uniform in style but commensurate with the importance of the customer? What are the milestones involved and who are the people responsible for the overall preparation and readiness?

There is a further aspect to the need to engage the customer in strategic areas. It is a simple well-known idea that sales teams must do good homework about the customer and the opportunity. Besides customer's key strategies, organizational awareness and information relating to team composition, there is an encyclopedic list of things to know and to prepare for.

One classic approach will be to work backward from the goal of having an effective first meeting(s) with the customer (in case of new customers or new division or even a fresh new opportunity). For a start, assuming you are responding to an invitation for a potential sale opportunity (or even if your approach is proactive), how best would you like to spend the 30 or 60 minutes that you will get with a team of important customer managers? What background information do you need?

It would look like the following:

- *company essentials*
- *genesis of the project/opportunity*
- *raison d'etre for the project*
- *customer's likely goal (outcome, cost, etc.)*
- *your possible responses*
- *competitive landscape for the opportunity*
- *key learnings from previous transactions with the same customer or a similar customer in the same industry space*
- *changes in customer organization and potential implications for your company*

- *customer's business performance at brand or category levels*
- *recent financial trends*
- *market news, brand news*
- *customer's recent successes and failures in the marketplace*
- *likely questions, likely irritants, likely follow-up process and so on*
- *possible steps involved in the buying process*

If a sales team can predicate these to a substantial extent (and I am absolutely sure they can), imagine the course of discussions and how you can control and steer it. Conversely, if the homework is poor, such meetings would get spent only in filling the information blanks. Besides, your lack of preparation will be palpable to the customer who could potentially rank you lower in their consideration set.

It is a strange reality that while we have increased retail consumer watch manifold with new tools like analytics and big data, B2B customers are not subject to the same rigor of information gathering. Much worse, companies are comfortable living with low visibility. The reasons are not hard to find. This is a time-consuming and skillful task which many account managers are not trained to do or have disinclination to do.

Data Mining as a Sales Skill

The question may arise as to how this task can be accomplished. Data mining is as much a habit as a science. Good salesmen do a few things well—continuous contact with the customer, catching whispers in the corridors, asking questions to confirm potential or gather basic quantitative data, discussing what-if scenarios with the regular contacts that can provide clues to upcoming projects, tracking media activities, asking customers pre-meeting questions to clarify issues and even bouncing some ideas on the phone or informally, depending on the relationship enjoyed. 'Most companies begin the process of gathering data to estimate their share of customer's business by simply having their salespeople ask the customer for this data. Bank of America Corp.'s Global Corporate and Investment Bank (GCIB) group and National Gypsum Co. have used this direct-query approach for almost a decade. And senior managers from both firms report that more than 90% of the time, customers respond promptly with accurate figures.'[3]

---

[3] James C. Anderson and James C. Narus, *Selectively pursuing more of your customer's business* (*MIT Sloan Management Review*, Spring 2003).

Good account managers also keep a record of such 'informal' discussions or data gathered. We always went one step further than a standard due diligence process. Our team would write the whole project brief (as anticipated from the customer), generate internal views and prepare a mock-up presentation of ideas and products, which could be fine-tuned based on further information from the customer, closer to the meeting date. In some cases, more than one scenario was contemplated so that we didn't leave anything to chance. Creating 'new' demand in B2B context is not easy, but you can shape and time the demand to your convenience if a strong homework culture is embraced.

As part of their homework, our sales teams would also engage with junior managers in the customer organization, not to snoop but to understand operating level issues and compulsions. These junior managers do not often figure in the 'team' definition but have substantial operating knowledge of processes, priorities, constraints, cost parameters and potential solutions, among others and may even be invisible influencers.

Many of our interactions, especially with multinationals, took place with brand and marketing teams. In order to enhance the marketing viewpoint, we trained our account managers in 'brand management' by including presentations by experienced marketing staff from our customers. This filled the minds of account managers with the marketing thought process, considerations, decision tree, brand lingo, brand positioning or re-positioning and analysis of implications. In some situations, we used parts of the *brand report card*[4] framework or other brand health evaluation techniques. We even appointed people with brand management experience from our customer industries to marketing or sales positions. By doing so, we mimicked our customer's knowledge, frame of mind and tactics so that the utility of our homework is better aligned.

One of my clients, a large packaging and label manufacturing company, had to ramp up their customer portfolio virtually overnight as they bought a state-of-the-art label printing and processing machine to cater to high-quality applications. They came up with a list of about eight medium-to-large customers who they wished to engage with. However, entry barriers were high as these customers had entrenched suppliers. The account management team picked up market samples of the products of these targets and sent the labels to the in-house technical team for their assessment and for comparison with

---

[4] Prof Kevin Lane Keller, *The brand report card* (*Harvard Business Review*, January–February 2000).

quality specs offered by my client. In two cases, they found that the customers were not receiving cutting-edge quality from their current suppliers. Armed with this data and analysis, the account team had little problem in opening the door for a couple of pilot projects, which led eventually to the start of a strong relationship with one of the large targets. Applying the concept of pro-active work, putting in the necessary homework and the meticulous execution, all contributed to a business possibility that otherwise looked bleak.

If you are pitching for a large retail banking software business of a bank, imagine the benefits if you have studied their branches, ATMs, customer-facing processes, even retail customer reactions or opinions and so on and used the knowledge in discussions with the CIO. A good grasp of the operating landscape of a target customer and analysis of the gaps is a very good starting point to make a target sit up in your initial conversations. In another case where a global technology company was trying to cross-sell to a gold-financing company, the account manager came up with a new product idea of a prepaid 'debit card' for usage by the borrower during 'settling down' period following transfer to a new place of work (often in a new country). The company adopted the idea, as it found a 'convenience' product, based on the security of gold or other assets pledged in the home country. The salesman had done a thorough homework of the different client segments, their 'money' needs and current products available in the market. This study offered a logical progression to gap analysis and new product ideas, even before it was solicited by the customer.

Your Homework Must Be Done by—You!

Salesmen may wait for such insights to be given to them by their internal partners (like marketing, sales support or insights departments), but it may not happen promptly and efficiently or it may be superficial. Our sales teams would routinely visit supermarkets to track customer brands, the shelf arrangement practices, consumer habits and so on. Where feasible, salesmen spoke to the store managers or the customers to uncover latent issues or buyer behavior, not captured otherwise in formal surveys. In our experience, this was definitely a key competitive advantage we enjoyed vis-à-vis our competition.

Customers are not always polite. You may have heard of incidents where customers abruptly stop sales presentations as the content does not reflect their realities. The tolerance for being off the mark can be very small in some cases and this arises primarily from inadequate (or mistaken) understanding of the customer's situation. Customers do not wish to waste their time. The worst consequence is that such customers are lost forever.

Be the Customer's Scribe

One of the hallmarks of a very successful account manager is his or her ability to write a project brief or an opportunity paper on behalf of the client. If the account manager knows the client deeply and if he or she has done extensive homework, he or she is in position to either fully write or help customer write their brief. To be called upon to do that honor is a recognition of the account manager's value to the customer. Besides shoring up your reputation, it always provides a checklist to customers and acts as an idea paper for them to ponder. Customers tend to lean on such account managers if they have noticed such skills in them. There were many situations in which our account managers managed to achieve that.

The homework concept extended to in-house activities as well. Account managers were encouraged to create internal agenda either in anticipation of a new opportunity or to prepare for a new initiative with a customer or a group of customers. Account managers utilized this opportunity to understand the strengths and special capabilities of our own organization and to devise 'entry' strategies into new accounts, armed with insights, analysis and potential solutions to identified problems. Many consulting and technology companies utilize the services of their in-house 'industry watchers' to write 'white papers' that provide analysis of one or two segments of the industry, its key challenges and solution approaches. If account managers can absorb these well and juxtapose on their knowledge of the customer, these are often the seed for account managers to take to customers to sow in their minds and seek new opportunities.

As important as the scope of customer data for projects or opportunities is, it is a basic minimum requirement that account managers know the customer's decision journey—the steps, the players, the criteria, normal duration, bidding process, external evidences or backing, veto considerations and so on. This would certainly vary across customers and perhaps even between divisions of customers. There is a simple tool used in services marketing that can be adopted here—'*blueprinting*'.[5] The blueprint,

---

[5] Valarie Zeithaml, Mary Jo Bitner and Dwayne Gremler, *Services Marketing* (sixth edition, McGraw-Hill).

similar to a project Gantt chart, not only lists activities leading to a sale but also the interconnections, sequences, vendor interventions and actors. It can also be extended to have time dimension for each activity so that account managers can try to manage that as well. Most good CRM software have such features. As the process is seldom fixed, it is vital to do frequent reality checks. If the relationship is excellent, the customer will help you with this.

3.3   KEEP THE CUSTOMER MOTIVATED DURING THE WHOLE BUYING PROCESS

Have you encountered situations when promising leads die suddenly, especially after making good progress? Is your sales team guilty of benign neglect of the customer when things are not happening? Do salesmen drop potential sales opportunities by digressing frequently? Is there a powerful locomotive in your system that keeps the customer engaged with you, even during lull periods in the relationship?

It is not uncommon in the B2B space for deals to take months, if not years to fructify. In the fragrance business, we had experiences of the first business coming in after as long as three years' painstaking effort. It is true of the software industry, medical equipment industry, industrial steel pipes industry, plastics, construction, aircraft, defense equipment and others. It can be a long and frustrating process with many highs and lows and with uncertainty all along the way. The process may not flow evenly as spurts and lulls are common. In as much as it is inevitable for sales teams to be fully engaged in the process and, in fact, be the driver of it, it is also crucial to keep the customer motivated. Salesmen sometimes tend to shift attention to other projects and not retain sufficient focus on projects that seem to move slowly. Their 'absence' from those projects signals to customers that they can sit back as well. While it is a natural tendency, companies must build in processes to ensure that there is a customer touch-action on a regular basis (meetings, correspondences, sharing of information or prototypes, etc.).

One of the methods we followed was to milestone projects. All projects were divided into four to eight key stages and timelines defined for each stage. Sales supervisors will track the movement in each project from stage to stage. The IT system alerted us about projects that stayed at the same stage for a period of time, usually for 90 days. This was a trigger to go to customer and ascertain progress or revitalize the project.

We introduced other measurement steps. We successfully built in a % revenue potential factor into running projects. If a project reached a certain level, it could be counted at 30% of its value in the pipeline calculations. (Project pipeline value was a metric used for salesman evaluation). With progression to each subsequent stage, this weight increased to 40%, 50%, 60% and so on. A project with a potential of $4 million brought a pipeline credit of $2 million when it reached the 50% mark (a 50% stage denotes some serious progress). It was thus in the interest of salesman to keep the projects on a 'moving trajectory'. This also meant that the customer was also tagged along in the same trajectory and that events of some worthwhile kind were occurring with regularity and the customer remained an active partner in such projects. During our half-yearly or annual reviews, salesmen took the opportunity to get customers to reaffirm the prospects and the scope of the projects.

Bringing Value to Customers Must Be a Constant Endeavor

In order not to make it a mere 'hey! what's happening?' kind of interaction, we trained sales teams to bring supplementary information or samples or presentations to rekindle the interest (and sometimes, act as reminder to the customer). There were other benefits of the progress pipeline system. It would easily call the bluff if a salesman clogged the system with 'imaginary' projects. It also facilitated comparative performance evaluation of salesmen. Further, every now and then, a supervisor would ask to go and meet the customer along with the salesman, in order to verify real projects versus ghost projects. It may indicate lack of trust, but it acted as a deterrent even if errant salesmen were only a few. In a few cases, we actually found that there was progress happening at customer's end, but that we were out of the race and this was not disclosed to us, or it was convenient for the salesman to keep it in the pipeline without jettisoning it. The only caution in doing spirited follow-up is not to err on the side of stalking, which customers hate (and salesmen would be given hints).

We need to discuss the concept of 'closing' here. Projects or sales opportunities are considered closed if there is a business win or a loss or discontinuance. Account managers have the responsibility to bring projects to a logical closure.

Sales literature offers several techniques to ask customers for an order. Some account managers become tongue-tied at the closing stages. They just cannot bring themselves to ask for the order. They may also miss buying signals. We trained our account managers on closing signals and techniques, among others, so that they don't miss the moment. Depending on the industry, such signals could include fixing dates for trials or market tests, discussion on lead times for product delivery, sharing of order patterns from the customer, submission of final specifications, payment terms, scheduling of a 'final' meeting with a decision authority and so on.

Managing Impending Closure

It is elementary but I was always surprised that many lack the skills or attitude to get a customer to write out an order. Some customers would delay the announcement on closure when they aspire for better commercial terms or keep the alternative option warm until the last moment. If you can sense this tactic, it is within your scope to fish out the intentions and address them squarely. In most situations, a delay may lead to revision in the evaluation of options and if you are ahead in the reckoning thus far, it could be a dangerous ploy to wait. An early closure also provides more time for your company to process the order and get production-ready. In some cases, an order is accompanied by advance payments, which has a cash flow implication to the operations. In situations where the order value is significant or in the case of capital equipment or software applications, there is usually a contract-writing step after the closure. This can take time and involve further negotiations on the terms. Going by all these considerations, it is ideal to close early and account managers should be skilled up for it. In many situations, you are perhaps one tantalizing step away from the order, but you do not realize it (or you fail to see the signals).

Accountability for Your Efforts

Organizations spend a lot of internal effort, time and money working on sales opportunities that salesman bring. Many times, this is done in the face of competition for internal resources. Hence it becomes critical to make the customer (and the account manager) accountable for investment in these projects. We had to walk away from a couple of customers when we discovered a pattern of opening new projects but not closing them. In the fragrance business and in many other businesses, pre-sales effort is not billed to the customer and is only paid back if it results in business. Like the venture capital industry, the successful projects pay for a disproportionate number of unsuccessful ones. Account managers, in their eagerness to clock new sales, should not allow 'less serious' customers or projects to exploit this privilege. If monitored with a good system, the percentage of 'real' and 'realizable' projects can be dramatically improved and wasted investment can be minimized. Of course, in some situations, we can treat the dead project as a learning tool, especially if it involved a new customer, a new category or a novel product or service idea.

Do You Know Why Your Projects Stall?

We realize that projects can stall and this can be attributed to many people and circumstances on both sides. How do we ensure that we understand the reasons and therefore can manage them better in the future? It is a good practice to evaluate salesmen in terms of closures and failures in closing. This will identify patterns that may need intervention by way of coaching or separation, after repeated failures. At every stage, it is useful to analyze the reasons for 'long pauses' in projects and perhaps even discuss it with customers (this will increase their accountability for the outcomes). In the fragrance industry, it was sometimes noticed that customers would retain the work done up to a point (copies of documents, samples, research findings) and promise to get back later. This is a tricky situation. You do want to give the customer what they ask for but do not want to be left out of the game when it resumes. In cases where it is unavoidable, salesmen should cultivate the practice of an effective 'temporary closure' and ensure that the next steps and the timing are clearly agreed upon with the customer. Account managers, in their eagerness, may fail to get agreement on the next steps.

Managing projects that move slowly or take too many twists and turns is far more challenging than projects that run predictably, at a steady pace. One of the tactics that worked for us, was to review 'sticky' projects separately as the deliberations will need greater ponder and creative solutions to reboot these projects.

Make an inventory of projects or opportunities that started promisingly but did not finish in the past two years (or longer depending on your specifics). Identify the reasons (the real ones, not account manager's hunches) for the stalling or discontinuance. In hindsight, what steps could you have taken to push the projects forward toward completion? What lessons can your account teams draw from this exercise and what process enablers should you build in for the future to minimize death by neglect? How can you make your customer accountable for closure of projects within a reasonable time? The answer will lie in industry practices and ensuring that customers are 'signed on' to the various activities at every stage.

3.4   BUILD EXTERNAL OR THIRD PARTY EVIDENTIAL SUPPORT TO YOUR PROPOSITIONS AND CLAIMS

Are you sometimes challenged by your customers to back your claims with independent evidences? Does your sales team have the skills and tools to convince customers of benefits from your product or service, based on acceptable proofs and protocols? Does your company leverage credible performances and benefit claims that can be authenticated?

Every company in an industry will fortify the sales arguments with testimonials, field test results, market successes, independent rating studies and the like. Given the possible large value of orders and the criticality of the product or the service, there is usually only one chance given to vendors. This idea is thus well known. Where products are not identical but the benefits are meant to be, choosing a product can be a tough call for the customer. You could use fragrance A or fragrance B for a brand of shampoo, for instance. The two products will smell completely different and yet may be acceptable to the consumers in the target market (like choosing from two or three qualities of wines that taste differently or two different flavors of ice-creams). Similar examples are aplenty in all industries. You can buy a sales software from Siebel (now part of Oracle) or from SAP or from salesforce.com. They are different in most aspects except that the end benefits will meet the needs articulated by a customer. Performance ingredients, medical process equipment and devices, office furniture, computer hardware, steam boilers, aircraft engines, market research services and many such industries fall into this category. Besides explaining advantages and disadvantages, what else could be done to reinforce your arguments? What evidence will pitch your product or service differently from that of the competition?

Your product or service may not only be challenged by your customers. It could be your competitors who do it for your customers. Vendors competing for the same opportunity are often expected to articulate a comparison of their product or service vis-à-vis direct peers. It is often an opportunity to 'play down' a competitor's advantages. But, external evidences will quite easily blunt such a sinister intent.

We sometimes resorted to an actual consumer test to demonstrate superiority of our product offering—among consumers of our customers (as we operated in a B2B2C space). Even though we did not know submissions from other competitors for a particular opportunity, we would seek consumers' responses to our proposed products vis-à-vis market benchmarks identified by the customer. We have won several businesses as a result of this strategy, based on successful test results. The consumer research was often done by the same agency that our customers would use and based on similar research protocol as the customer. This ensured credibility for the exercise and the results. We would even get the research agency to come along and present to the customer. This demonstrated not just that there was a winning fragrance in the pack, but also our willingness to back ourselves by investing in consumer research and showed our ability to understand deeply the end consumer market and preferences. This tool was often used when entering new customers or new markets.

It is important, however, to be able to delve into the research findings (or other corroborative studies) and understand the fine 'lines between lines' to find the right arguments. It helped us that we could either read the report as an expert or had people with such skills in the team.

One of the examples is etched in my memory. We were pursuing an opportunity to fragrance a detergent brand in Vietnam, belonging to a multinational. Our own consumer research threw up exciting results. It is common for researchers to focus on the mean (or average) score of a product and to measure how significantly it beat a benchmark (using statistical standard deviation methods). We found from our study, however, that the top box score for one of our options was very high. Fifty-four percent of the consumers, who used our test product, rated it as 'extremely suitable for the detergent' and that they 'liked it extremely'. This kind of a high score at the top end of the rating scale is unusual. We verified it through scores from other attributes and made sure we were reading it correctly. When we met the customer, we dived straight into this statistic and brought it to the customer's attention. The director ordered for a technical trial of our fragrance straightaway. We sold the fragrance to the company soon thereafter and for a few more years. (It was a special achievement since we were not an empaneled supplier.) This demonstrates that customers would not want to lose out if there is compelling third-party evidence of consumer benefits that can boost their brands.

One of the world's largest market research companies uses 'case studies' as supporting evidences. If a customer problem looks identical to another situation that they had handled, they present the other case (depending on confidentiality terms, the other customer may be named or disguised) and the solutions provided in that case, with the question 'would you like to consider that kind of an approach?' The market research company had many tools for different research needs, but instead of offering the tool as a product, they found it sensible to offer it as a solution that worked elsewhere. Credibility was won with that reference instead of merely parading the product. (Many customers like the solution language rather than the product language.) Consulting companies even publish 'case studies' on their websites or in their regular newsletters that can address known issues or proactively surface hidden problems of customers. This is used as a powerful technique for lead generation. Depending upon the industry, it is therefore beneficial for a company to create a bank of case studies covering a variety of problems and solutions that the company was associated with.

In recent times, there is the much publicized story of a Japanese airbag-inflator maker.[6] The company was named for supplying air bags that caused fatal injuries while inflating and this affected reputed carmakers like Honda, Toyota and Chrysler. The airbag maker eventually agreed to form an independent review panel that would help the company navigate the problem and identify issues to tackle on a permanent basis. This is a way to win back lost credibility by building external review or certification alliances.

The software industry is a unique case in point. The vendors keep discovering new solutions or extensions as every customer's problem could throw up a new challenge. In order to extend the usefulness of such new development, the vendors agree with the customer (sometimes contractually) that the customer would oblige if asked to provide referral to another customer. For non-standard products or services, nothing could be better than a testimonial from an existing happy user.

---

[6] http://fortune.com/2016/06/10/the-takata-airbag-recall-is-now-a-full-blown-crisis/.

Authentication = Credibility = Positive Reinforcement

Building credibility through external 'authentication' serves several purposes:

- It shores up what may otherwise be seen as a weak proposal or challenges/counters a new vendor's credibility.
- It can address naysayers' doubts (among the customer).
- It can act as reassurance for your internal support team who participate in the project (as external endorsement is a powerful testimonial).
- It can boost the confidence of account managers in their early years at the job.
- It creates a better understanding of what stands for a solid 'proof' of the pudding by neutral users or organizations.
- It is a starting point for objective assessment of your products or services (and challenges customers who evaluate subjectively).
- It is a good demonstration of the stakeholder intentions of your company, as you invest in securing such external evidences or testimonials, without the guarantee of a sales outcome.

Other forms of evidences could be user experiences, user surveys, visits by prospective customer to factories or laboratories of existing satisfied customers (software applications or new technologies), endorsement by independent rating agencies (like JD Power), product trials in actual use conditions (automobile components) and others. In as much as your competition could adopt the same strategy, possible points of difference should be explored. From an account manager's point of view, it is important to develop a good understanding of these supporting evidences rather than merely distribute printed product materials. It is possible that building user-evidences or third-party endorsements are under the jurisdiction of a support team and not the account managers. Even so, it pays for account managers to be trained in these arguments as you sometimes get only one chance to attract customer's attention or initial interest.

To ensure that this offers relevant and unchallenged competitive advantage, it is vital to mimic customers' use conditions in the tests and perhaps even seek an agreement on how the tests or external validation would be done and results measured. You need the customer's buy-in for the methodology and for interpretation of results. Building this benefit into your account management process calls for investments and must be a conscious long-term decision. In some situations, once the credibility is irreversibly established, companies may be able to walk away gradually from external validation and move to only customer trials and other forms of self-certification (think Rolls Royce engines).

3.5   CREATE A PROACTIVE AGENDA, BOTH INSIDE AND WITH THE CUSTOMER

Have you had situations, where you were caught unawares of a large sales opportunity and had very little time to respond? Does your sales team engage in planned activities that are based on opportunities that they sniff from a distance? What is your company's process for 'getting battle ready'? Does your inside team have the full picture of looming or target opportunities that your sales teams may be privy to?

One of the problems of a hectic business cycle is the limited or no readiness to face briefs, projects, sales leads, tenders or opportunities. Many companies do not have mechanisms to consciously manage run-up to projects. It may not provide sufficient head start even if you reckon you have a well-oiled sales or project machine. Unfortunately, the subconscious effort may not be good enough in all cases. If the project or brief is a 'competition' or a 'meet', the readiness program is the training 'trials'. Would you compete in a major 100-meter sprint competition without adequate preparation and training? Olympians toil for four years for the brief few minutes on the D-day of the event. In the military language, this is like building up dry powder in readiness for combat.

Abraham Lincoln (1809–1865) said, 'If I have eight hours to chop a tree, I will spend six hours sharpening my axe'.

We extended the concept to our business and created a pool of activities called 'proactive projects'. Professor Vijay Govindarajan calls it the 'planned opportunism'.[7] It is akin to training horses for the race in 'race-like' conditions. The proactive projects were defined and run exactly like a real project from the customer, except for information like target price which we may not have had at the time of kicking off a pro-active project.

---

[7]Vijay Govindarajan, *The Three Box Solution* (Harvard Business Publishing, 2016).

We made the account manager a co-owner of the project, which in effect meant that key project information as relevant to a customer or a group of customers had to be plugged in by them. The concept is not very different from Malcolm Gladwell's 10,000 hours of honing skills, propounded in his best seller, *The tipping point*.[8]

Many times, these proactive projects also happened to be the target sales opportunities for the account manager. Proactive projects also entered our project pipeline IT system and progress was monitored exactly the same way as we did for customer projects. Given the short turnaround that is often the case with customer projects, the proactive projects ensured that all internal people put in their best efforts, with time in their hands. Whenever we lost a business, it was reinitiated into the system as a 'recapture' project. It was sometimes difficult to motivate people to work on such projects that did not always lead to a sales result. Here again, the pure sales based incentive system comes in for questioning. We built in a suitable weightage for completion of proactive projects while measuring salesmen performance. There were occasions when the proactive projects formed about 40% of projects that the company was working on and by corollary 40% of the resources were deployed. That is a serious commitment.

Proactive agenda also led to healthy competition from account managers for internal resources and attention. Only the best-defined and projects with the most chance of a customer brief within sight got into the internal work plan. It was also expected of the account manager to establish a clear vision for the project and to 'sell' it internally. In conversations with competitors, we got to know that they did similar things as well. However, there were key differences. The ownership, the reward linkage, progress monitoring on par with customer projects were some subtle differences that meant a whole new outcome from these. It is important not to let these projects become second or third priority work for everyone.

Involve the Customer in Your Proactive Work
What is the role of customers in your proactivity? There are two broad types of customers when it comes to engaging with vendors at a pre-stage. One group is very willing, wants to be part of it and will provide resources and information to help you. These are newer players in the industry and those who have reaped the benefit of this approach in the form of innovative and pathbreaking solutions. They also view this as saving valuable time and energy in their own interest (especially if they are resource-tight).

[8] Malcolm Gladwell, *The Tipping Point* (Little Brown, 2000).

The other group may think that this is a waste of their time and resources (they see this as helping you more than them). This group may also be doing its own homework before a project and would want a minimal interface at this stage. They may be 'consuming' a lot of content before getting prepared to face the vendors. In some ways, they will reach step three or four in the sales journey, on their own. But you can engage with them too—by providing important content that feeds into their information appetite. As these customers may have a strong desire to own the 'pre-assessment', any relevant information that your company can provide not only enhances their expertise on the subject (that is one of their goals) but positions you as an informed supplier worthy of engagement. In today's digital world, this should be a piece of cake for a vendor, even if the content is to be somewhat tailored.

There were also instances when our company presented the proactive project results to the willing customer and used it as a route to seeking an opportunity in an upcoming brief. If the results are strong, no customer will turn you away. In a few cases, we even got an 'exclusive' opportunity, based on the quality of the proactive work. A company willing to put in a lot of time and resources into a yet-to-be-commissioned brief does impress a customer of its bona fide intentions. A leading global software company has been winning a staggering 90% of all its proactive projects as they are ahead of competition in those cases.

Proactivity is also a mental frame of mind viewed from an individual standpoint. Account managers with that aptitude will clearly lead over others. Stephen R. Covey, in his landmark book *The 7 Habits of Highly Effective People* opens with 'be proactive'[9] as the first habit. 'Businesses, community groups, organizations of every kind—including families—can be proactive. They can combine the creativity and resourcefulness of the proactive individuals to create a proactive culture within the organization.'

Your Proactive Work Can Help Customers Prepare Better

The other benefit of proactive projects is that we compensated for customers' sloppiness in time planning. In our context, customers often underestimated their go-to-market time duration and squeezed all activities including a fragrance choice as launch dates approached rapidly. Working proactively provided both of us a buffer.

---

[9] Stephen R. Covey, The *7 Habits of Highly Effective People* (Simon & Shuster, 1992), 77.

As mentioned in the 'wants' chapter earlier (Sect. 1.3), many customers seek consulting and advisory support, especially before they evaluate solution options. This role requires vendors to deliver a 'well-processed' thought paper on the customer's situation and possible solution matrix. Proactive agenda management will smugly feed into such consulting engagement with customers. This model is adapted from the management consulting industry's practices.

The results of the proactive projects depend entirely on the 'quality' of work put in. In my conversations with some senior software salespersons, I offered this suggestion as a route to stay ahead of competition. Many of them concurred that they were doing something similar but lamented that the internal teams including technology people and pre-sales teams never gave the required attention and the end result was not robust nor was the organization truly ready for the battle.

You Could Dictate What Should Come Next
The IT industry is a classic case in point for the need to do this. In the 90s and subsequently, customers decided the shopping list of what applications needed to be introduced or revamped. They set the agenda of implementing an Enterprise Resource Planning (ERP) or an accounting or inventory platform. Software vendors lined up to serve the need and walked out when the job was done. In the past decade, however, IT companies revamped their approach. They analyzed their clients' needs, their current system adoption levels and offered a road map for other potential systems or upgrades along with due business justification. Thus the initiative shifted from the buyer to the seller. This enabled the sellers to plan for the opportunities rather than play the waiting game and respond to them, if and when called. This has resulted in a dramatic change of fortunes for the whole industry, with more predictable order flows and activity cycles. The leading technology company, Infosys, introduced the concept of 'Zero Distance'[10] with their customers in 2016, symbolizing the degree of closeness they desired with key customers and thus exhorting the account teams to do everything that is needed to get to a zero gap.

One of the world's largest banks has a formula for its relationship managers who deal with corporate clients in Asia. They have stipulated that only one-third of the time should be devoted to transactions. The remaining time should be divided between planning for new opportunities with the

---

[10] www.infosys.com.

customer (generating new agenda of cross-selling and upselling projects) and planned relationship engagement. This is a good thumb rule but needs self-discipline from account managers to follow. Their natural preference is for transactions and routine relationship chores, often with a few 'friendly' customers.

The next time you wish to target a large piece of business from a customer, write a proactive project, convince the internal teams and track the outcome. The biggest advantage this brings is that the output is customized and does not follow a cookie-cutter approach. There is a great chance that your customers will value your company for this effort that saves them time and money on pre-feasibility studies and helps them to start at step three or four instead of from scratch.

If you are dealing with customers who are innovative and introduce new products with keen regularity, this approach can be blended with innovation brainstorming (internally) and you may be able to go to customers with a package of ideas, ingredients (or equipment), cost structure, branding ideas, market positioning, names, among others. Our marketing team was thus often involved in generating a set of whole new ideas that may be relevant to a customer's category or product line. Innovative ideas need time to evaluate and presenting them early to customers gives that extra slack. This approach was useful in opening doors to certain customers or individual categories where we could not claim expertise in any other way. Account managers were thus encouraged to don their thinking hat and generate customer-relevant product innovations. This was an important value-add for most customers and in many cases led to the 'wow' factor that we were seeking in order to establish enduring points of difference.

It is a common myth that product innovation ideas are the prerogative of the 'technology or technical' departments. You will be surprised to know that even the smartest marketing companies are sometimes yearning for new creative consumer-relevant marketing ideas. A large market research company was involved with a tire major for the introduction of a new technology with premium benefits, positioning and pricing. The tire company not only accepted their research findings but also adopted their brand name suggestion for the product. Companies like Procter & Gamble have a policy of seeking out and collaborating with external parties who bring in new ideas to their product portfolio. Working proactively also gives you some amount of license to parade your own pillories, when compared to an invitation to a brief or an opportunity which may be more straightjacketed.

3.6   SHARE KNOWLEDGE GENEROUSLY WITH CUSTOMERS

What is your company's philosophy for sharing comprehensive knowledge with customers, on a sustained basis? What process in your company supports your philosophy? Do you often find yourself in situations wherein your customer is vastly underinformed than you are about your products or services or the applications? How do you get the customer to perceive value in knowledge that you share?

Even in the era of abundant free information on the internet, customers do not acquire the same amount of expertise as your company. But they would like to. The boon of the internet is its bane. Information on 'tap' is not always relevant or concise or, worse, authentic. This is the era of DRIP (data rich, insight poor) information glut. B2B buyers, as overwhelmed as they may be, are too smart to just depend on such unverified sources or generic information. 'Too many sellers have wasted millions of dollars on sales technologies such as CRM systems and data warehouses that never lived up to their potential.'[11] Thus good information is scarce, hidden and may be elusive. Further, in multinational companies, managers move around and find themselves in businesses or categories, which they need to learn ab initio. This presents an opportunity for your company to share knowledge with the customer managers and even accept some responsibility for educating them.

Why Share Knowledge?
The primary aims of informing and educating customers are:

a. *To fulfill the appetite of customers for information on a variety of things that impact the purchase. Younger managers have a propensity to consume content prodigiously.*
b. *To articulate the vendor's expertise in the product or service*
c. *To subtly promote the vendor's products or services*
d. *To act as a continuity platform of engagement with potential and actual customers*

[11] Andris A. Zoltners, PK Sinha and Sally E. Lorimer, *How more accessible information is forcing B2B sales to adapt* (*Harvard Business Review*, January 6, 2016).

e. *To dispel wrong notions or understanding that customers may carry (concerning the product or service) by offering an authentic version*
f. *To prepare customers for actual pre-sale interactions and evaluation*
g. *To enhance satisfaction from product or service use through 'correct' usage education*
h. *To stimulate interest and demand for new products, virgin technologies or innovative solutions*
i. *To ensure that successive line of customer's managers will keep up with the vendor's identity, credentials and active engagement*
j. *To act as a springboard for customer contributions to your content generation or to new product pipeline*
k. *To provide soft 'goodwill' for the vendor at the background.*

There is another powerful benefit that vendors seem to miss—it's the synergistic output of ideas shared. Says Steven R. Covey, in his famous book, *The 7 Habits of Highly Effective People*, 'You begin with the belief that parties involved will gain more insight, and that the excitement of that mutual learning and insight will create a momentum towards more and more insights, learnings and growth'.[12] Vendors thus stand to learn from their customers and vice versa.

So clearly, more information shared is better. It is not that companies are not aware. However, it is interesting to see what practices are actually followed. Many companies have training and orientation programs for their key customers. It usually relates to products, processes, technologies, end-user benefits and so on. Some companies arrange factory tours for customers to familiarize them with production and quality control processes. But the information demands have gone beyond. What you do must enhance the customer's expertise significantly.

We tried to make a difference by offering seminars, which we otherwise offered internally, especially technical seminars. We did not feel threatened by customers acquiring similar scale of knowledge as we found that the goodwill generated far outweighed any fear of leakage of secrets. A well-informed customer is a delight to transact with. Account managers were also encouraged to share openly information that was in their domain.

It was routine for our teams to share market knowledge, trends, industry forecasts, consumer behavior, shifts in buying patterns, category adoption

---

[12] Stephen R. Covey, *The 7 Habits of Highly Effective People* (Running Press, 2000), 264.

rates, trends in fragrance preferences or dislikes and so on. Sometimes, customers had similar or better information. Yet, this helped in ensuring that we kept pace with customer's knowledge and simultaneously developed greater clarity on these, based on the discussions that ensued such sharing. Customers assess the competence of vendor managers on the basis of knowledge they bring to the discussions. It is, in fact, a surrogate for your company's competence as well.

Customers are always curious to know how they stack up in terms of prices they pay for the products or services. After all, this has been their primary turf in the past for garnering savings for their companies. We sometimes shared ballpark prices that the customer industry paid for products from us or from our competitors (ensuring no confidentiality is breached). One of our large customers treated it in a fair manner and was even willing to pay a bit more sometimes for what they rated as better products or better overall service. The notion that sharing cost or price puts you at a disadvantage is often a myopic view. Customers either know it already (and are only seeking to confirm with you) or they treat such information with maturity. In industries where products or services are not identical, this comparison is not easy and account teams need to consider apple-to-apple pricing references.

If you are in an industry like software applications for banks, this could be translated to sharing of information on software status in the banking industry with highlights of best practices (without necessarily naming which of their competitors was on top of the curve), technology or benefit trends from across the globe, cost benchmarks for similar applications (customer would also get their own insights), future forecast of extensions to applications, emerging customer and consumer needs and so on. Some large technology companies employ researchers to use past and current trends in a vertical (or industry) in order to extrapolate the next frontier of customer needs and solutions. These research or white papers are highly valued by customers for their future orientation. Such information would surely trigger a dialogue with the customer and if steered well can lead to sales opportunities. This is even more useful in a dynamic industry like information technology and in situations of frequent change of customer personnel.

It also needs special efforts to customize the knowledge mix for different customers. Thus, newsletters and bulletins can help to some extent, but customers tend to undervalue such mass distributed documents. Sadly, however, account managers engage only in addressing customer's articulated needs and seldom go beyond a holistic knowledge exchange.

Customization Is More Beneficial
The greatest benefit of our sharing information was that customers took a couple of steps forward and shared more information than they would normally have done. We were often privileged to be taken through customers' business plans, invited to internal discussions or marketing launch events, given advance copies of advertising campaigns (and sometimes asked to give opinions) and were even involved in M&A ideas and plans. This was akin to a board seat. It was a confirmation of our ability to mirror customer's interests, the high trust we enjoyed, the knowledge sharing mindset and our competence to engage in a consultative dialogue. What better way to demonstrate that we believed strongly in and embraced 'stakeholdership'? If you are seen to be open and willing to engage beyond the contours of 'commercial gains', it tells a good story about the genuine motive of your engagement. If your information is customized and contextualized, it is even better.

While there are many examples from my experience, I could easily cite this one. A large global consumer brand in the health segment was being given a makeover by our customer (brand owner) and the objective was to modernize it and take it to a higher value positioning. The brand had been a low-priced no-frill one for decades. We were involved in early discussions on possibilities of such higher positioning, justification platforms, cost and price implications and so on. We offered one of our ingredients to deliver additional properties to the core proposition. The deal did not conclude for a number of reasons, but we strengthened our position with the customer in the course of these joint discussions as we demonstrated capacity and willingness to engage in business-relevant dialogue, offering a range of additional information and analysis. Over time, our team made it a habit to share information that added a 'delta' value to the customer's own sourced insights. Two things are important to achieve this—a good understanding of the customer's businesses and an armory of business-relevant knowledge and insights to share. It comes with experience and a bit of lateral thinking. More importantly, it flowers in company environments where such outreach are actively encouraged. Companies working in silos often lack the impetus for building such skills as critical information seldom trickles to the man in the last mile. It is common in large corporations for employees to hear about important happenings in their company from the public domain including media.

Exploit New Communication Technologies

The digitization of information all around has made some of these tasks easier. Customized data and information decks are now possible to be shared online through private or semi-private online communities. Some companies have gone further and created a two-way online dialogue that stems from information or trends shared. It is a cost-effective and powerful way of stimulating advance discussions on emerging needs or challenges and possible technologies and templates for solutions. A digital platform for high end sharing and two-way communication with customers will soon be a basic feature of knowledge transfer. Some member of the account team must be entrusted with the responsibility of being the 'page owner' for updates, responses and conversations.

Companies like GE have taken the knowledge sharing principle to a higher level, by providing technology trends and so on (www.ge.com). They also have professionalized the editorial responsibilities with experienced scribes. Platforms to host content on behalf of companies are now on the rise. Companies have also started to create 'online feedback communities' of customers who are encouraged to share their experiences, problems and ideas. This provides an automatic pipeline of issues for vendors to examine and deal with. Webinars are part of other new tools to engage the customer in new knowledge sharing. Some of the communities encourage customer-to-customer sharing as well. This also builds up goodwill and word of mouth support for the vendor. Customer forums and communities are indeed the surrogates for advertisements in the B2B world. In the next ten years, more millennials are likely to move into positions of responsibility and decision-making and this is the only way they know to work with external partners like vendors.

As an implementation step, develop a framework for knowledge nuggets to be shared with your key customers—newsletters, white papers, online two-way conversations, technology forums, webinars and so on. Create appropriate delivery support to execute these and get the account managers to track its implementation and customer feedback. If your tracking is good, you may even be able to establish the correlation with leads generated or projects won.

3.7   DEMONSTRATE COMMITMENT TO YOUR CUSTOMERS' RESULTS

Are you willing to link your fortunes to that of your customers? What is your company's attitude to the idea of vendors being rewarded or penalized based on customers' achievement of results? Do your customers sometimes voice dissatisfaction that your products or services are not pulling enough weight in their pursuit of their goals? How do you sensitize your account teams to caring for the customers' results?

The true concept of 'stakeholdership' is when customers do well and your product or service plays its part in that achievement. This is the underlying hypothesis of 'creating value' for the customer. It is even more so when your product or service is directly related to your customer's performance in the marketplace (ingredients, machinery, advertising campaign, packaging, etc.). However, in most situations, there is only an indirect influence. In B2B2C contexts, it is possible to assess the impact of an ingredient or a marketing component (like advertising) on customer's market performance. There may be other metrics like cost reduction, faster factory throughput, lower product rejections, manpower reduction, reduction in process time, increase in consumer convenience, efficient data capture, optimization of resources and better consumer experience that can be attributed to your company's products or services.

We had a diversified customer base consisting of local and regional players who thought more like entrepreneurs at one end and large, professionally managed global corporations at the other end. The ability to think like an entrepreneur and a professional at the same time was a skill we (and our account managers) needed to master. Another of our very large customer, with whom we managed to develop a business size equivalent to about 70% of their wallet in a short span of about six–seven years (the customer attained No. 2 position in market segments they operated in), had the promoter family of two generations running the operations. With every brand we fragranced, our capability (and future opportunities) was assessed more or less on the basis of brand performance. We were fortunate that most of the brands did very well in the marketplace and exceeded customer's expectations (by a factor of two or three sometimes). Most of our discussions centered around customer's market performance vis-à-vis their competition.

The market metrics sometimes included market share gains, dollar sales and even profitability, even though we did not directly contribute to the profitability of the product, except in a small way. Our conversations always involved brand performances, changes over the past months, performance of other competing brands and so on. Our concern for the customer's results was demonstrated frequently, not just as superficial discussions, but based on thorough data analysis.

Results and Metrics to Align with

The obsession for customer's success can begin quite early in the selling process. Tom Magnuson, CEO of one of the top ten hotel chains, "recalled a success story of a salesperson who walked up to him after a presentation: He said if it wasn't a good time, he could leave a document with me. He pulled out an envelope and said that his team had spent nine months analyzing data on 1,000 Magnuson hotels and had ideas on how we could increase room rates and brand ratings for each hotel. This was presented in a couple of sentences with a simple graph on a bar napkin. Within weeks, we signed a chain-wide software agreement with that company".

The salesman was successful because he knew what Magnuson needed and provided insights about his hotels. *Don't just tell someone that 'I want your business.' That's like telling them you just want their money.*[13]

In the advertising industry, it is now emerging as a practice to link campaign fees (compensation) to product performance, at least in part. Top advertisers like P&G and Coke, over the past decade, have ushered in 'value-based' compensation or 'pay-for-performance' model, where a significant part of the agency fees is linked to brand performance. Some of the annual maintenance contract fees for equipment are linked to 'uptime' metric. In some industries like civil construction projects and hotel management, the link comes in the form of a bonus or penalty if targeted outcomes (including time adherence) are met or not met. Copier companies now install software in your copier network to track usage by each user and can present comparative charts of copies or prints done by each authorized employee. This even comes with historical charts and dollar implications. The companies are also able to capture savings from previous vendor arrangements, based on data provided by the user company. In the medical

---

[13] Frank V. Cespedes, Jay Galeota and Michael Wong, *Salespeople need a strategy for selling to CEOs* (*Harvard Business Review*, 13 October 2016).

electronics field, companies such as GE and Siemens track significant data on usage, time efficiency and so on by installing software as part of the equipment. These metrics cover operational, strategic and financial areas that help the hospitals and clinics track the performance and optimize and fully exploit the benefits of such equipment.

GE, for instance, provides such benefits via its iCenter through extensive monitoring and diagnostic services to its oil and gas customers.[14] Many logistics and supply chain providers have introduced 'apps' that help customers keep track of performance, efficiency or productivity gains and financial benefits attained, from usage of their products and services. Technology is thus at the forefront of enabling either self-monitoring by customers or quick monitoring by vendors, without human intervention.

Success fee is now very prolific in a lot of digital services and platforms. One of the startups in the area of e-commerce has a solution to identify and track 'chronic' product 'returners' who return part of what they buy online. This company, besides charging a subscription fee, asks the online retailers to pay a success fee when their return rates reduce, as a result of weeding out the obvious culprits.

This Is the Future Era

Such concepts can easily be extended to many other industries. This is an emerging phenomenon that will force companies to more directly align their prosperity with that of customers. Account managers will need to develop skills and versatility to analyze customer's performances, link the impact of their products or services to such performance outcomes and to join discussions with the customer in brainstorming sessions and even offer solutions based on an external perspective. While technology can provide data dissected in different ways, insights become the responsibility of the account team.

Aligning with Individuals' Goals

It is also useful to align with the individual goals of managers at the customer's end. In large professionally managed companies, young managers would be eager to show quick strides in results. If you have the opportu-

---

[14] www.genewsroom.com/press-releases/ge-launches-industrial-internet-solutions-predictivity™-and-its-kl-based-remote.

nity to help them in this endeavor (with your products or services), you stand a good chance of a long and enduring commercial relationship with the customer through the manager.

We had the opportunity to interact with a technical manager of a large multinational company who had just assumed his new role in a new country and was eager to get on with the game. One of the 'holy cows' in the brand portfolio was in need of rejuvenation but nobody dared to do much about it, since it was also a cash cow. This manager engaged us in a dialogue and our first task was to feed his curiosity and interest in knowing almost everything about the creative process, ingredients, selection considerations and the industry. The actual project followed soon and our product displaced a longstanding fragrance, albeit through a rigorous competitive process. This was considered a 'coup' at that time as many competitors had set their eyes on that business for a long time. We were fortunate in this instance, to align ourselves with the professional agenda of one of the managers.

That the relationship between a vendor and a customer has acquired a symbiotic dimension is now well acknowledged. As a result, new emerging concepts like appointment of a 'customer success officer' are in practice. This is a good beginning and an acknowledgment that this is how the future will look. However, all account managers will need to play this role and the customer success officer may become the repository of information and the source of tracking 'success' trends rather than the 'creator' of success for customers.

The sharing nature of the relationship between Motoman, a leading supplier of industrial robotic systems, and Stillwater Technologies, a contract tooling and machining company and a key supplier to Motoman, is a more exemplary one. 'The two companies are so tightly integrated that not only do they occupy office and manufacturing space in the same 165,000-sq-ft facility, but their telephone and computer systems are linked, and they share a common lobby, a conference room, training rooms, and an employee cafeteria. Even the animated exhibit in the lobby is a joint endeavor: a trio of robots that perform for visitors during an entertaining narration on the capabilities of the two firms. Push one button and you get the Motoman spiel; push another and you learn about Stillwater-and its role in making parts for the robots. The small robot in the middle serves as "emcee" for the presentation.'[15]

---

[15] John H. Sheridan, *An alliance built on trust* (*IndustryWeek*, 17 March 1997).

Vendors and customers have even morphed into joint ventures where each company invests capital, in order to fully reflect the intertwined fortunes of the two sides. This ensures long-term commitment to mutual results and can lead to greater cooperation in aspects like innovation, new technology adoption and new business models. In the automotive industry, for example, component manufacturers join hands with vehicle manufacturers to set up dedicated companies and production lines. This is also a case of the vendor's willingness to sink their teeth into the business of the customer and to align the financial fortunes over the long run.

You may wish to start with an exercise of self-rating on how much your product or service is impacting your customer's top line or bottom line or other measured parameters. If your rating is above five on a scale of one to ten (ten being very closely aligned), you must initiate a tracking system that can measure the cause (your sales to the customer) and the effect (change in customer metric) for certain chosen periods. This could be an eye-opener for many companies if they come to realize that the effect is not positive (i.e. your products or services did not do a good enough job to improve customer fortunes). You may also do similar exercise for your direct competitors to check if they made better contributions. This will be a wake-up call!

3.8   Don't Take Eyes Off the Customer, Even if You Have Lost a Business

What does your organization do when you lose an existing business or a new opportunity that you competed for? How do you continue to engage the customer without allowing for a vacuum? Can you redouble your efforts to position yourself for the next opportunity?

Qantas Airways ran its historic Sydney–London flight with a stop-over in Singapore for over 60 years. In 2012, however, they terminated the alliance with Singapore's Changi Airport and chose to move the stop-over to Dubai. Five years later, it was announced in August 2017 that Changi Airport has won back the transit arrangement. That is a big achievement for Changi Airport that they could reverse a sad loss in 2012. That is the triumph of the 'never give up' spirit and keeping a high engagement agenda with customers even when it appears that you have been consigned to the wilderness.

We do not win every business opportunity that we compete for. We may even lose some after looking like winning. Our company may have put significant energies on an opportunity without returns. What do we do when we are faced with this loss situation? We have two clear options— move on from the loss or stay put to pursue it again or to pursue another opportunity with the customer. The default option for many companies is the former. This approach has the following implications:

- Knowledge and insights developed during the lost project or business is wasted
- The momentum built with the customer is surrendered without capitalizing
- Customer intensity with the specific customer is allowed to dissipate
- You end up going back to the beginning of the queue
- You lose ground, not just an opportunity

The nature of the fragrance business is such that companies encounter wins and losses all the time. Existing businesses are frequently challenged by competitors and if brands are ready for a makeover, fragrances and suppliers may be changed. This is the popular musical chair story. This situation exists in many other industries too. In the software industry, the tenure of a major business application is perhaps five–seven years, as technology keeps leaping forward (the life may even be shorter for smaller modules). There are hardly any industries that do not have healthy competition in the B2B space. There are very few life-long or permanent businesses. There should be no room for complacency when you are an incumbent supplier. Equally, there need not be long grieving for a loss. In fact, you need to redouble your efforts when you are sitting out of a business. In the fragrance business, it was common for companies to initiate a 'recapture' project, to be ready for the next round, similar to what political parties do (or are supposed to do) when they get voted out.

Seasoned account managers will tell you how the hunger for getting back a lost business can be stronger than chasing a new business. The sting from the loss should be productively deployed to learn the lessons and reshape the strategy. Ask any mountain climber especially those who seek out to climb peaks like the Everest. They rarely succeed at the first attempt. However, with every failure, they get better. Their problem identification and solution mindset improve and their resolve gets more intense. They zero in on mistakes and work to eliminate them. They re-equip themselves better and their anticipation of hurdles is sharper. In many cases, the focus becomes even more single-minded. That kind of missionary zeal is sometimes harder to bring out in sales situations though, but why not?.

I cannot claim this to be a unique achievement of my former company as the industry, in general, had such practices. Our learning was that competitors could use different strategies from the incumbent to gain a foothold where they don't have one. This becomes the catalyst for the vendor change. Price is one ploy but there are others as well (technology story, compelling market evidence, pedigree and global adoption are some). In fact, we tried to reverse our roles and would tell the team to think like competitors and aggressors in order to get the edge needed to reclaim lost business. Our strategy to claim a competitor's business was even called an 'attack' strategy. One of the other guidelines we used was to balance continuity and change when attempting to reclaim a lost business. As readers would recall from the best seller book, *Who Moved My Cheese*, change is a powerful ploy to retain your edge and in many instances the only one. Our internal tagline was to look at renewal opportunities as 'evolution' with a big 'E'. Sometimes it becomes our duty as a supplier to handhold the customer toward changes that are beyond incremental 'tinkering'. Moving between generations of servers is different from taking a leap forward to cloud solutions, for instance. That may be the route to recapture a lost business.

Complacency that leads to a loss or retreating after a loss is equally dangerous. In the software industry scenario, for example, if you do not assess the 'state-of-the-art'-ness of your customer's outcomes (not processes alone) vis-à-vis their competitor or the best practice in the industry it may hide the need for new steps. If account statements prepared by a bank for their customers have an error rate of 0.4% while the best in class achieves 0.1%, you know you need to help your customer (the bank). As standards keep improving and as end-consumer demands keep evolving, companies need to keep pace suo motu. This is similar to the proactive culture we talked about earlier. In addition to helping your company raise your guard, customers do appreciate the 'paranoia' that you show in safeguarding their interests relentlessly, even when the chips are down. That appreciation will translate to the votes that you will look for when it matters.

Staying in Despite Setback Is a Better Strategy

The recommended strategy when you lose a business or an opportunity is thus to 'stay' in the customer actively, nurture other opportunities and the relationship, without loss of intimacy or momentum. It is harder to reclaim these if you step away (ask competitors who are trying to get in). Smart customers notice these developments instantly.

Irrespective of current performance with projects and businesses, there is the question of long-term engagement and stability. We frequently employed a tool that measured the stability of our relationship (or vulnerability in an opposite sense) with major customers. The tool was developed with our trainer and it involved several parameters that included the following:

- *our efforts*
- *outcomes*
- *relative standing versus our competitors in a defined time period*
- *share of wallet*
- *complaint rates (disputes, if any)*
- *number of substantive contacts/relationships in the customer's organization*
- *percentage of opportunities received in a time period (if the customer initiated projects worth x million dollars, what proportion of that was briefed to us)*
- *number of praises/compliments received*
- *referrals made by the customer*

Notice that these parameters go beyond the revenue and profitability goals. When compared with scores of a previous period, this would tell you the direction and magnitude of change, both positive and negative. If done honestly (as most of the ratings are somewhat subjective), this can trigger action areas for you to step up the game. We would often remark lightly that our anxiety increases with wins and not losses—the anxiety to safeguard the business.

Do a stability analysis for your key customers, map the trends and identify reasons for significant change. This would convincingly point to issues like 'reduced' engagement, train of losses, benign neglect and so on—aspects mostly under your control. If there are several customers in your portfolio showing declining stability, it portends unequivocally to lurking business dangers.

3.9   DON'T PROMOTE A STRICTLY TRANSACTIONAL APPROACH

> Does your sales team have a bias for immediate orders, even if it is of strategic low priority? As an extension, do you find it difficult to motivate sales teams to pursue long and multi-step deals with high potential? Do you have situations where a large part of the organizations' resources is plowed into just filling the 'order bucket'?

There is an inherent conflict between the natural tendencies of a salesman and the company's interests in an account management context. We clearly understand that the goal of B2B businesses is to develop a customer base and relationship with which we can build enduring businesses and maximize the share of wallet. This automatically means that we are interested in *the total basket* rather than individual pieces of business or transactions. For the typical salesman, however, any order from any customer is welcome, especially if the performance metrics are aligned with dollar sales with no regard for the composition.

There would be a mix of highly profitable products or services and medium or low profitable products or services that may have to be offered to the same customer in a classic account management construct. The willingness to live with this dichotomous situation will determine if you are correctly exploiting customer potential. Due to various reasons like customer's own variation in profitability of different business lines or product categories, varying budgets in different years, product life cycle impact, customer's competitive pressures and your competition in specific products , his ability to pay will vary. In our business, customers had brands that stretched from luxury to economy segments with consequent implications on price affordability and volumes. Tom Peters once said, 'Treat the customer as an appreciating asset'. The total basket approach builds on this philosophy by aiming to fully exploit all the benefits of 'owning' that asset.

How Do You Measure Profitability?

We had a product line reporting of profitability at some point. This came in the way of the total basket approach and was rewarding the transactional approach. For example, a customer with a sales revenue of $200,000 with a gross margin of 50% looked much better compared to one with a sales revenue of $1 million with a gross margin of 33%. The latter customer perhaps bought several products, with varying turnover and margins. The product line margin obsession clouded the account optimization game plan which is fundamental to a well-run account management program.

We switched to customer level profitability analysis and it was loud and clear to account managers that they can add new businesses to their portfolios of existing customers without insisting on same product margin every time. The only danger in this premise is that account managers may 'overuse' this concept and drag profitability down with every new deal. This can be easily dealt with during periodic account reviews with the account managers and by stipulating that opportunities above a certain value need price clearance beforehand.

The B2C Approach

There is some similarity with B2C industries like airlines, telecom companies and banks. The loyalty programs of these industries are also built on the principle that it is more advantageous to sell more to the same customers and that every transaction is not necessarily profit accretive and resource optimizing. Some credit card companies provide deep discounts of up to 20% on gas bills, for example, which may not be profitable as an individual item. In recent times, many telecom companies have switched their focus from merely increasing subscriber base to improving 'ARPU' (average revenue per user). They have evolved multiple strategies for upselling, cross-selling and introduced the 'family customer' concept to extend the fruits of an existing relationship. All industries have their own pattern of economies of scale, which therefore act as the motivation to shun a pure transactional approach. (Companies in their early stages of the cycle may still aggressively pursue customer acquisition and transactional approach, but as they move up the cycle, they will realize that this has limitations to achieving long-term financial rewards.)

ABC Analysis of Customers
A related principle is the ABC analysis of customers. Most of you must be familiar with the concept that your customer base can be divided into three or four groups depending upon the size of business (revenue, profits) that they do with you. 'C' is usually the group that is smaller or less profitable or both. Companies who adopt the 'basket' or the 'share of wallet' approach, carefully

scrutinize the 'C' group to ensure that it does not grow like the dinosaur's tail and may even prune it from time to time. One of my bosses used to call this 'firing customers'. In the era of treating customers as kings, this is not the ideal term to use but is an inevitable tool. This is also sometimes catchily referred to as 'shrinking to grow'. If you want the best bang for your buck (your time and other resources), you need to choose appropriate customers to work with, cross-sell and upsell more and more to them. Major banks continuously evaluate their corporate portfolio to re-position customers as priority or non-priority based not only on potential but often based on risk profile. Thus the exercise can lead to 'dropping' some customers and pushing the business up with some others. A pure transactional approach may lead banks to higher exposure to a risky customer that they actually want to de-prioritize. Thus, who to sell to is often a more important question than how much you sell.

The total basket approach also has a self-fulfilling character to it. The more you sell to a customer, the more you get to sell to that customer. This philosophy has to be ingrained in the way account managers think, act and behave. The higher the wallet share you have with a customer, the easier it gets to improve on it. Top account managers can do this almost as a second nature. The training company, 'Mercuri Goldmann India',[16] a company in the Mercuri International Group, uses a concept called 'brick-walling' to denote the stranglehold you need to develop with your target customers, which will raise switching costs for your customer and make it harder for competitors to come in. If you can do it by serving customer priorities as well, you have a powerful winning formula.

The Route to Acquiring Scale

The difference between small technology/software companies and the giant ones is that the latter get better and better at cross-selling and upselling to existing customers that the small companies get edged out of major deals and sometimes have to sell out as they struggle to build scale. Size and dominance that come from maximizing wallet shares can also lead to strategic gateways like mergers and acquisitions.

Another practice we followed in order to wean away from transactional approach was to view margins in absolute terms rather than in percentage terms. Depending on the industry, this is a more than useful tactic. If your

---

[16] (www.mercuriindia.com), October 2017.

pricing per product unit (or weight or order or other units) sits in a large band, it makes sense to look at absolute margins. For example, if you sell $100 per unit as well as $200 per unit products, you may accept a margin of $50 from the second product, compared to $35 from the first product. If viewed from the percentage angle, you may find it unacceptable. Assuming it is an incremental business to an existing large customer, would you let the business go if it came at lower percentage margin? For all you know, the lower margin business may be a potential blockbuster and you don't want to be left owning the eggs rather than the bird.

Companies desirous of embracing high-performance account manage-ment should do two things:

1. *Analyze your customer base and decide which of the 'C' customers you want to drop so that resources can be diverted to the more priority customers. (Tip: choose the lowest profitable among C customers first, then the higher profitable but still small customers or the customer with declining revenues in the 'C' category.)*
2. *Analyze the past 30 or 40 (or another significant number depending upon your industry) sales orders received and determine their contribu-tion to increasing wallet share of existing customers. If you have more than 50% of the orders not contributing to higher wallet share, your account management strategy isn't working well and needs tweaks. (Cross tally this with the lost orders from existing customers and this could be a tell-tale finding that you are pushing for new sales at the cost of winning more from existing customers, the opposite of what is recommended.)*

3.10   DON'T GO UNDER COVER IF CUSTOMER FACES PROBLEMS THAT LEAD TO YOUR DOOR

How do you deal with situations when your customer has a problem and you have contributed to it? Does your account team possess the skills and methods which assure the customer of your sincerity in solving the problem? How do you ensure that such incidents do not leave ugly scars? How do you recover lost goodwill, if any?

When some airbags of Toyota, Chrysler and many other cars inflated and resulted in some deaths, these car companies were in deep crisis. They had to recall the vehicles (a staggering 30 million, by some estimates), investigate the problem, handle the public ire, deal with regulatory agencies and contain the damage to their carefully cultivated safety images. It was proved subsequently that the fault lay with one of the suppliers of the airbag. It was not clear if the supplier came out clean immediately (otherwise the recall could have been contained). Whose image suffered the most here? What lessons do we learn if we imagine ourselves to be the bag supplier?[17]

Your customer needs you more when they are in trouble. And if it happens to be due to something that your company failed to do or could have done, it is imperative for you to be fully visible, proactive and responsive. Even if it is only remotely connected to your product or service, it provides a golden opportunity to earn brownie points if you stand shoulder to shoulder with your customer.

Empathetic and Swift Response

This again is an obvious point but customer relationships could start to slide unknowingly if, in the customer's perception, the vendor has been less than supportive. The absence of the account manager at the time a problem is discovered delayed acknowledgment of the problem, poor quality of response or remedy, any hints of unwillingness to accept consequences, invoking commercial terms to drive home the seller's limited liability, diverting the customer to a third party (who is involved in logistics or other functions) are some of the reasons that could result in bad blood with the customer. Inexperienced account managers could add fuel to the fire by their lack of empathy with the customer and using legal or offensive language in communication.

It is conceivable that most problems arise from mistakes on both sides. And yet, in the interest of the long-term relationship that we seek with the customer, we have to take a step or two forward to douse the fire. This is often a tipping point that could pave way for entry of new competition.

We had numerous instances of this, small and big, and our attitude was always positive and proactive engagement with the customer. It is even becoming the norm for vendors to assume the risks of the vagaries caused by external factors.

---

[17] https://www.bloomberg.com/news/features/2016-06-02/sixty-million-car-bombs-inside-takata-s-air-bag-crisis.

Back in the days of slow truck traffic and no mobile tracking systems, one of our trucks met with an accident and our customer's plant was going dry due to delayed delivery of our supplies. Even though it was essentially the customer's fault in not maintaining sufficient safety stocks (and not informing us about their new inventory policy), our team jumped into action. We dispatched one lot by a passenger train (as they travel faster than cargo only trains) and sent one of our staff with the consignment just to make sure things did not fall through the cracks. The customer greatly appreciated our extraordinary act of ensuring smooth plant operations. Such support may be common in some industries, but there are often gaps between what is written down in manuals and what is practiced when the crunch comes. In most cases where customers get to a point of annoyance with the vendor, the reasons are slippages in 'timeliness' and 'quality' of response. Customers do have some tolerance for other aspects (including how the costs incurred in solving the problem can be shared).

There is a strong virtue in putting such issues to bed quickly. The longer the time you take for bringing in effective mitigation, the more irritable the customer can get and the stronger the likelihood that the issue lingers on as a sore thumb. A few such instances can lead to the decline in customer intimacy that we desire.

We also learned a lesson that it is prudent to have a plan B whenever possible, as customers don't always factor in uncertainties. Account managers were encouraged in our company to suggest ways to redress the problem quickly even if it meant some additional costs, as customers seldom forget these. Opportunities for mishap or malfunctioning or a failure are more common in computer hardware or software industries. The companies usually have 'response time' commitments but one too many slow responses will jeopardize long-term reliability scores. In our experience, customers can also see through excuses that are offered for slow responses. So don't even try.

The Paradox of Failure

It is now a popular theory that you can actually improve your standing with customers when you make mistakes, provided the recovery is timely and handled with care. This is the 'paradox of failure' and is especially true in service industries or where service is an important component of a business. I am not sure if the social media obsession in B2B businesses is as high as the B2C domains. Good feedback (of a well-redeemed failure) or bad feedback shared in public space can have a big influence on how other customers view your company. Customer communities and forums can easily spread these messages quickly, causing impact to your reputation.

When there is a failure of some sort and you get around to addressing it as a true 'partner', it is advisable to bring it to a formal closure. Many times account managers move on to their other priorities without doing this. The issue may resurface on another occasion if it has not been properly sealed. It is like the wound which was never properly sutured. Some customers may even demand an after-the-event inquiry into how the incident happened and seek remedial actions to prevent recurrence (if it was your fault) and even financial damages. Vendors should not shy away from such examination, as it is also in their interest to track the root of the problem (it may even prove customer's guilt in the bargain). If done well, this may help eradicate the root cause of the problem.

The next time you encounter an incident that leads to some suffering or anxiety for your customer, do a postmortem of the incident and draw conclusions. If your relationship with the customer is strong, you may even want to share the findings with the customer. If you do not have a protocol for dealing with such exigencies, this may be the right time to write one. Lay down clearly the responsibilities, response times and escalation rules in such a protocol and avoid ambiguous language. The protocol should also deal with how to communicate with the customer as you manage the crisis and bring it to a closure. Account managers need to be trained in implementing such protocols in letter and in spirit.

3.11   Support the Compositional Needs of Your Local Organizations

What is the balance between global managers and local team members in your country sales teams? What are the criteria that you adopt for determining local organizational needs? Do you have a situation where local units are over-dependent on handholding from the global pool? How do your key customers perceive the competence of your local teams?

Sales organizations start to get more complex when you are in a global industry and have global and local customers. You need the global expertise while maintaining an optimum local touch (remember that account management is a high-touch approach). In a global business, it is always a catch-22 when to consider local managers for positions of responsibility and when to parachute global employees. With respect to account managers, there is sometimes a slight bias in favor of local talent, due mainly to language considerations. However, the assessment should go beyond just the language. There is a cultural and a human resource angle as well. Local managers clearly understand corporate and individual culture and behavior very well and this is hard to replicate.

The German industrial major, Siemens 'required all global account team members to undergo intercultural training. It believed that to be successful with an account, you needed to interact with the customer based on gaining significant knowledge of its country's culture. According to David Macaulay, Siemens' Senior Vice-President of global accounts, 'one of the keys to our global success has been our acceptance of different cultures. If you don't understand cultures or are not sensitive to another person's culture, doing business can be twice as hard'.[18]

Why Local Competence Matters?

To a large extent, it is also a question of how you want to build your human resource strength. Would you like to build an organization that taps into locally available talent as a first choice and therefore there is a home-grown entity with accompanying ethos? As account engagement is a long-term strategy, what is the best sustainable human resource model? Local management has to be weighed against the practice of seconding global managers to do local roles that many corporations have followed for long. If managers of your customers are largely pooled from local sources, it makes eminent sense to pitch for a local bias in your company, as the two sides must establish deep relationships through their managers.

One of my friends and a senior at B-school heads a top global market research agency in Indonesia. He is an expatriate, but over a period of about five years, he converted his entire team into local executives, investing heavily in finding the right talent and grooming them. He claims to have created a significant talent pool, equal to any other organization, in a country that is not always exposed to global practices.

---

[18] H. David Hennessey and Jean-Pierre Jeannet, *Global Account Management: Creating Value* (Wiley, June 2003), 217.

My former company's Asian sales operations were led by a local manager in every one of its 11 subsidiaries. Besides, about 95% of the other managers in account management were local nationals. Our key competitors would often have global expatriates in many positions, but we stayed with our strategy. It paid dividends in the form of early maturity of local organizations and in developing pride in themselves. The pride was a key source for people retention, as our talent stability in key markets like India, Indonesia, Thailand and Korea was almost 100%. Training, orienting and mentoring were continuous processes deployed to achieve the perfect alignment across country organizations. In subsequent years, these local talents were even exported to developed markets. It was harder to take this longer route but the results were very satisfying. One additional benefit, even if it was not the motive, was in containing manpower costs and keeping them aligned with the country-specific cost and price structures.

Our greatest challenge came from China. The team had to be built on local lines, in view of many country, society, dialect and provincial peculiarities. It was challenging to assemble enough account managers of the right caliber that we needed. Even more challenging was the choice of the head of the account management team. We had a virtual merry-go-round with a new head appointed every two years, including even a German with substantial mainland China experience. All moves largely flopped, as evidently we did not have the right mix of human resource. A relative success was a local manager who was internally groomed. Though he got his dues a bit late, he rose to the occasion. I have heard many of my peers in other companies talk about the talent difficulties in countries like China. Traditional selling was the predominant skill available in China at that time. It was nevertheless important for us to show faith in our local talent strategy and pursue it even if results came later. To escape this, companies try to junk the philosophy early and bring in too many global managers.

As countries show tendencies to practice veiled protectionist labor practices, this would even become a necessity. Strangely, the more globalized the world is, the more localized is the labor force. Global companies with global customers face the daunting task of offering seamless standardized account management experience, overcoming country and people differences. This problem has not been fully solved in Asia.

The availability of trained manpower skilled in English and local language has shown a big improvement over the decades. In the franchised food industry, big names like McDonald's and Starbucks have created the same service experience across several markets by suitably training up the local talents. This should encourage B2B companies to also look for ways to integrate local managers into their organizations. If the philosophy is embraced, ways can be found.

In your sales teams for different markets, you may wish to make a beginning to consider predominant local managers. To achieve this without compromise on company results, you will need to invest heavily in training and coaching. Some companies draft experienced global managers for short periods (of, say, six months) in order to preside over the transformation and to ingrain the company's culture and account management practices. This is a wise move with a long-term payoff.

CHAPTER 4

Skillsets and Knowledge (of Account Teams)

4.1 ACQUAINT THOROUGHLY WITH YOUR STRENGTHS AND WEAKNESSES

> What are your relative strengths and weaknesses vis-à-vis key competitors in vital areas relevant to your business? Do you have a clearly articulated position on these? Are the account managers familiar with that position? Do they practice active propaganda of that position on a sustained basis?

A company cannot be all things to all people. All companies have strengths and weaknesses. Whether it is a first sale or a continuing relationship, correct articulation of a company's position is critical. These are not always published or shared even internally in a concise way for employees to internalize. An account manager has to make an effort to understand these, absorb them and benchmark vis-à-vis competition. In that respect, this is a skill that needs to be acquired based on a good knowledge of strengths and weaknesses. In our experience, front-line managers like account managers are the least informed about key strengths or weaknesses. An account manager cannot afford to be unaware of these in depth. He or she needs to do this as homework for his or her own benefit. Many times, the repeated projection of strengths fortifies the brand image in B2B, as there is no other way to create a clear brand proposition.

© The Author(s) 2018
B. Shankar, *Nuanced Account Management*,
https://doi.org/10.1007/978-981-10-8363-1_4

Strengths can be leveraged in sales arguments. For example, if an organization has x number of patents in a product category or a field, it has positive connotations of being a technology expert. Knowing and understanding this aspect, even briefly, does help in loading your side of the scale in discussions with customers.

I once worked at a steel company that had the best technology, process expertise, equipment and application knowhow to make a certain category of high precision tubes known as 'cold drawn welded' tubes. The company had the leading market share in that category, miles ahead of the second competitor. It also had years of experience in application technologies for many performance-critical applications. However, neither the technological superiority nor its high market shares were mentioned in any of the marketing collaterals like brochure and product literature nor were account managers in the habit of highlighting these in customer pitches and conversations. The distinctive capability was important to crow about, as the company was also in the business of low-tech furniture tubing. In hindsight, I felt that the company missed the opportunity to garner 100% share of that segment that was more or less open for their taking. It was so superior in that segment.

On the other hand, some salesmen project such strength almost singularly during pitches. I was part of a customer team that was evaluating software for schools. One vendor marketed his company's product as one that runs in 1400+ schools. And only that! He had worked out that in software buying, reliability, customer base, years of expertise and the like have a significant bearing on the buy decision, especially if it is a packaged product for mainstream applications that does not need a lot of tailoring.

Strengths are real strengths only if your target customers believe you have them. Weaknesses are real weaknesses only if your target customers believe you have them. You should not attempt to list every single issue under each heading, just the +/− 6 most important ones. Every time I do this with a company, the weaknesses list is at least twice as long as the strengths – this is nonsense! Stop beating yourself up. The objective is not to list all the most important issues under each heading and then put the analysis away in a drawer! The objective is to do something with the results of the analysis. The organization's belief must be tested in the marketplace, to find out clearly whether the customers agree.[1]

---

[1] Paul Fifield, *Marketing Strategy Masterclass* (Butterworth-Heinemann, first edition), 25.

Know the Specifics

It is important to know the specifics of the strengths. For example, if your company is financially strong, it would be useful to know the basis (owned by ABC group, government-backed, has a capital base of x million, reflects a high stock multiple), the aspects of strength (cash flow, lower fixed cost structure, expertise in tender pricing) and, if possible, cases to cite. In order to be an effective tool, the strength and weakness analyses have to focus on areas that are relevant and have at least a modicum of influence on how the selling organization is viewed in terms of competence, image, legacy, leadership, 'cutting edge' and so on. This often requires some customization of the language based on each customer. Strengths of a company in the B2B space are often the source of brand equity.

During my days when I led the account team of the fragrance company, we would always tell our customers that we were (at that time) a family-owned and managed company in operation for over 100 years, with the fourth generation of the family at the helm. This had certain positive connotations of stability, long-term outlook, salience, trust, focus, renewal, evolution and reliability for customers. It also was sometimes perceived as a surrogate for flexibility in dealings (as opposed to a public company driven by short-term shareholder interests).

In a similar way, it is important to have a comprehensive understanding of what your company will not be able to offer. These are not merely the differences in product range or commercial terms but deeper aspects like limitations in technology, after-sales support, customization scope, supply chain constraints and so on. If you do not want customers to make wrong assumptions about these, it may even be prudent to spell it out to customers. As a rule, we would tell customers what mattered to them and what could have an impact on their expectation versus delivery. To some extent, this is an extension of the training to be able to say 'no' to something, even if cultural inhibitions sometimes stood in the way. Account managers are afraid of diminishing their chances of success if they brought in 'but' and 'if' into their sales arguments. In an era of multiple sources for corporate information, especially the internet, it is not advisable to avoid disclosure of relevant information that could be potentially uncovered by the customer in other ways. Large customers often have their own checklist of what aspects they would like to know about potential vendors. This will directly flow from the capabilities and limitations of the vendor's products or services. It's a bit like the health card of a potential employee. You need to know if there are health issues as you make up the decision to hire.

Know Your Competition

As a corollary, you must know your key competitors' strengths and weaknesses as well. Knowing how it differs from your company's will be a useful insight to craft appropriate strategies. If you know the 'chinks in your armor', it helps to develop counters to negate arguments from the customer, especially when your competitors don't have the same weakness. Midsize software companies, for example, often project their on-site resource capabilities as a positive difference vis-à-vis larger players who may tilt toward optimized on-site/off-site models as client engagement progresses. For many customers, the on-site 'buffer' is valued as a good safety net and resource for 'quick' fixes.

I once posed the question to a sales head of a leading technology company and asked about his two direct competitors. He could not articulate a single aspect of difference in his first recall. I reworded my question and asked 'why does your competition succeed where you are not able to'. He rattled about seven distinct reasons. I then asked him to do a strength-weakness analysis of his company and the two key peers. It took him half a day but he had an articulated document at the end. This is the homework that is often missing in many companies.

Why Account Teams Should Develop Their Version?
In some organizations, analyzing strengths and weaknesses is the responsibility of a marketing or sales support function. While they would probably collect, organize and articulate the strengths and weaknesses in lucid marketing language, I have come across account managers just parroting them (without the customization needed) or sharing the information through non-personal channels like emails or brochures. This is clearly a sub-optimal outcome. Readers would realize that emails or brochures are looked at only cursorily or not all. A personal presentation of this at the appropriate point in the sales conversation is ideal and would also necessitate that the account managers have a good grasp of the issues in order to stand the scrutiny of customers.

During your next sales conference, ask your senior account team to draw up a statement of strengths and weaknesses, as perceived by them, along with that of two or three direct peers. It should cover a maximum of ten areas that matter. This can then be linguistically polished to develop a standardized document for their use. (Please be prepared for some surprises in their understanding!)

Know *thy self, know thy enemy. A thousand battles, a thousand victories*—Sun Tzu (sixth century BC)

4.2   MASTER THE FINANCIAL IMPLICATIONS
TO THE CUSTOMER AND TO THE COMPANY

What do you know about the financial impact of your product or service for your customer? How can you mimic the calculations that your customer does before and during negotiations for a deal? What is the extent of familiarity your sales teams have for basic or intermediate financial calculations and application?

B2B sales transactions tend to have a major impact on the financials of the customer either in costs or in revenues or in investment outlays or all of these. A new piece of machinery, for instance, will cost the customer amortization, interest and operating costs while impacting the revenue arising from productivity, run rates and uptimes. Salesmen may have limited capability to understand and digest financial or economic information, given their educational degree or exposure. This is, however, a key prerequisite to being seen as a 'stakeholder'. A stakeholder needs to be able to link the product or service to some financial considerations and outcomes of the customer. If you can establish the linkage between your product or service and bottom-line gains to the customer in dollar terms, you could save a lot of hard selling arguments. It pays to not just understand customer's financial data but also acquire familiarity with some of their specific financial terms and metrics they use.

Total system cost is a term many multinational companies use, referring to all costs associated with buying a product or service from you. Print and copy machine manufacturers use the concept, 'total cost of ownership' (TCO). Similarly, many leading global companies have a practice of specifying the target cost per ton of their product, which means the supplier has the flexibility in terms of the price of the fragrance (per kg usually) and the quantity of incorporation in the product, as long as the multiple met the target cost of the finished product.

As we would realize in several of the chapters, account managers need to cultivate good 'data science' skills. Tracking customer's broad financials like turnover, profits, trends over two or three years, performance of individual brands and segments in dollar terms. Even market news and stock prices offer useful insights into strength or weakness of the overall financials (and hence possible intensity of price negotiations or the prospects of postponement or on-time project execution) as well as clues to product performance issues—losing share to competitors or weak market demand, among others. I have often found that the easiest argument with a customer is the financial payoff that is supported by a good 'gap analysis' based on financials.

Salesmen in the advertising industry often have to face 'budget cuts' of customers and hence postponement of campaigns is an inevitable tactic, as customers tend to treat promotion as 'discretionary' expenses that can be rescheduled if bottom-line considerations are paramount. Anticipating this could lead to your company coming up with alternative solutions to keep the revenues flowing and ensure continuity in the campaign, but with some short-term concessions or staggered implementation.

Help Customers Justify Your Proposal to Their Organization

Many customers (in fact, all) have a strong financial orientation and appraisal process for large purchases. Metrics like ROI, payback period, total system costing and economic value added (EVA) are often adopted to justify new investments and this process goes through the approval committees in the customer's organization. Vendors are often asked to supply financial data that is an integral part of such an analysis. While support can be sought from other functions like finance, it is a good virtue for account managers to be able to understand the process and contribute to the financial computation. In some government contracts, a financial calculation sheet is provided by the vendor as part of the tender documents. This sheet can be a complex one, depending on the product.

Each sale or purchase has financial implications to your company and to the customer. Mastering financials of the customer is an extension to understanding financial implications of each opportunity to your own organization. In large software companies, it is the norm for account managers to be asked to make a 'business case' for each project in order to be able to demand internal resources. This will very often consist of cost-benefit ratios and ROI metrics.

We trained our team to track and interpret some key financial information of clients, even though we were handicapped by the 'private' constitution of many medium-sized customers. Trends in revenue, profits and a few ratios like return on sales Earnings before Interest and taxes (EBIT percentage) or return on equity (especially relevant for banks and financial companies) or return on assets (for asset-intensive infrastructure companies) are very useful measures, especially if benchmarked vis-à-vis the customer's peers. In the case of new customers, these would also help in assessing potential for your product or service as well as any lurking credit risks. Some companies do a separate credit risk assessment, which needs to be signed off by the finance department, before business begins.

A good grasp of financial data and manipulation is also useful in price negotiations. I have always found some of the purchase heads to have an accounting background, and therefore, salesmen cannot be handicapped in such situations.

For example, in a software sales situation, if the customer is flush with cash, he may offer you an upfront lump sum every 12 months, instead of monthly payments. Do you have a reckoner to evaluate which is more profitable for your company or can you do a quick, back-of-the-envelope calculation to make that decision? Large companies tend to attach an accountant to the sales team to help with these situations, but that can become a crutch for sales teams not to skill up enough. Salesmen can get a better respect from customers if they are able to effectively engage in financial conversations as much as the rest of the sales process.

Necessary Skill to Cross-Sell and Upsell
In enterprise banking, the new themes are 'cross-selling' and 'upselling'. This means that banks wish to offer their full range of services to selected clients and this idea sits perfectly with the concept of selling more to existing customers—provided you can understand the financial needs of the customers. An educational institution that I advise as a board member moved part of their banking to another bank (bank B) that offered a high level of e-banking. All payments, including salaries paid to the staff, were shifted to bank B. This bank, however, over the past three years, has not tapped into the other needs of the institution. The salary bill runs into a few million dollars, which is transacted through bank B. Based on some estimation, bank B should have assessed that the fee collection is large and there is usually a cash 'float' as school fees are collected in advance. This is a lucrative business for banks as little or no interest is paid on these floats and they contribute to the bank's free-of-cost liquidity. The school has retained the fee collection transaction with its original bank (bank A) and the new banker is yet to realize this opportunity. It is even more inexplicable since banks now have a special focus on SME (small and medium enterprise) banking. There are two possible reasons—relationship managers

(account managers) are not trained to analyze available financial numbers to extrapolate new business possibilities or the bank has not yet embraced account management and remains a transaction player. In both cases, it is the bank's loss.

Cost Structures and Related Terminologies

Understanding different cost structures of your product—variable cost, total cost, overheads and so on—is very useful in tight negotiations. One of our multinational customers surprised us by offering to choose our fragrance, but at 20% discount to our quoted price. We didn't normally discount that much. However, this was a special case as it would have been the first entry into a mainstream brand of the customer, and given our substantial amount of work done to get that far, we were not keen to let it go. We had a relook at the cost sheet, which showed that at the customer's offer price, we would make a small profit but not lose, based on the variable cost level. We accepted the offer by trading for a minimum tenure. We then back-engineered the calculations to seek better terms from our ingredient suppliers and gradually improved the profitability of that product. Without the understanding that in marginal businesses variable cost is the one that you need to cover at the least, we might have given up that business and lost the entry opportunity. In fact, it got us some goodwill as we disclosed to the customer that we were compromising on our standard margins in order to begin a deeper relationship. That objective was also achieved eventually. I am sure many companies follow this style of 'entry pricing' strategies, but the concept of knowing price and cost boundaries at the account management team level is extremely useful.

While this could also be done off-line from the discussions and settled at a subsequent point in time, there is always a danger that a customer may alter the offer or procrastinate the decision, if given more time. Hence it pays to be able to nimbly handle these unexpected financial alternatives and propose or accept new options.

I do realize that companies are sometimes coy of sharing detailed cost data with salesmen for fear of underachievement in negotiations. Our experience was that given time salesmen grow up to manage this in a matured way for the benefit of the organization. Too many sales-based incentives can, however, drive salesmen to sub-optimal pricing. Incentives are matters for discussion, in a later chapter.

KNOW THESE… ideally

- *Cost of the buy versus benefits therefrom (for a customer)*
- *Cost of different solution options (yours or competitors' or of both)*
- *Internal Rate of Return (IRR), ROI on an investment project*
- *Financial analysis of customer's brands, businesses (leaders,* laggards, inefficient operations, productivity and so on)
- *'What-if' scenarios and their impact on costs, revenues*
- *Pricing options and profitability implications*
- *Total cost system of your solution—initial, recurring*
- *Financial implications of make versus buy options*
- *Financial implications of buy versus lease *or rent) options (in case of equipment or large initial investment products)*
- *Financial implications of solution or machine upgrade*
- *How to stack up dollar values of all benefits you offer?*
- *Financial implications of advancing or postponement decisions*
- *Sale and leaseback calculations*
- *How a major financial event at your customer (sale, acquisition, new funding, etc.) will affect your business or potential business*
- *Tax implications attached to your product or solution*

One of your customers has just reported a new acquisition of a smaller competitor. The company has declared that the return on capital employed will be impacted in the short term due to one-time cost absorptions and goodwill payments. The company, however, has confirmed that the acquisition will contribute positively to the return on capital employed after 36 months. You are the vendor of a key ingredient to the company (but not to the acquired company). Analyze in financial terms, the implications of this development to your business (hint: price pressures on your existing business that will befall in such situations versus new business opportunities in the acquired company).

4.3   DON'T SUBSTITUTE QUESTIONS WITH ASSUMPTIONS (OR PREJUDICES)

How good is your account team when it comes to gathering information from the customers? What is the existing skill level in the practice of logical questioning and eliciting critical responses from customers? What is the degree of comfort in professional questioning process? Do you have situations where the account teams plug in their conjectures rather than inputs generated from customers?

The closer you get to a customer, the higher are the chances that you know the customer too well. Even though you can somewhat predict customer's behavior or views in specific situations, it would be suicidal to prejudge customer responses. Every situation is intrinsically different—customer's current position, competitor activities, relative importance of the project, events that happened yesterday or during this week and a surfeit of reasons exist as to why customer has the right to modify his or her behavior. Account managers, therefore, cannot take customers or their opinions for granted. It would be futile to quote a previous instance to try to alter customer's response. If you need to judge a situation where clear customer response is not offered, your understanding of the customer could help in formulating one, but with suitable caveats.

The importance of 'questions' cannot be overemphasized. Many people think 'selling' is the same as 'talking'. But the most effective salespeople know well that questioning and listening are the most important part of their job.

As children, we demand answers to many of our questions, some very basic. When we grow up, that somehow gives way to assumptions about the answers. Account managers are many times reluctant to ask a basket of questions, as they think their customer understanding is challenged. This is not true. Customers are used to being asked questions and would rather offer clarifications than be misconstrued. Some account managers ignore this trick for so long that they become habituated to shun questioning as a beneficial tool. As human beings, we also tend to over-exhibit our knowledge or understanding even when asking is a better strategy.

Types of Assumptions
There are five types of assumption pitfalls:

1. *Assuming the buying process, dynamics, roles of managers or decision criteria*
2. *Assuming customer's cost targets or budgets*
3. *Assuming customer's potential responses to a product or service options and suggestions*
4. *Assuming that a 'negative' comment in the early stages is a 'rejection'*
5. *Making assumptions about the strength or weakness (or even existence) of competition*

Even a seemingly logical assumption on any of these could prove to be detrimental to the sale. In all the cases, a simple routine of questions and responses will add substantial clarity and factual evidence to the scenario. We sometimes had to force account managers to seek specific opinions rather than advance their own idea of what those opinions could be. Account managers can 'assume' too much in familiar cases.

Let us examine a simple routine of making assumptions versus questioning: A familiar customer has called you for a discussion for one of their upcoming projects. Here are the possible assumptions you would make in anticipation of the call:

The customer rarely calls on phone to fix up meetings. So it must be something urgent. It may pertain to one of the standard products that customer has bought before. Perhaps the customer may be calling one or two suppliers only because of the urgency. Price and timeliness will play key roles in the decision. Instead of these assumptions, if you had gone with an open mind and deployed the questioning technique, it could well go like this:

You:	*Thanks for your call. May I know the reason?*
Customer:	*We are looking at a revolutionary product to be launched in about 18 months. We do not have all the answers. We thought we would consult some key suppliers to gather more information on the ingredients.*
You:	*Sure. What is the product and what are your interest areas?*
Customer:	*The product is still confidential but I can share that it is aimed at delivering xxxxx benefit to consumers if used for six to nine months. We have some initial thoughts on the recipe. However, we are seeking independent formulae ideas with key ingredients that can deliver this benefit.*
You:	*Yes, we can provide that. What cost parameters are you looking at? May I know if you have a consumer price of your product in mind?*
Customer:	*We are not sure yet. But we believe consumer prices could be about 30% more than current products in the category.*
You:	*When would you need this information?*
Customer:	*Not tomorrow (!), but in three–four weeks?*
You:	*Absolutely! Thank you for calling us. If there are further questions, may I call you?*

As you can see, all your initial assumptions are wrong and the reality is quite the contrary. It took some simple unbiased questions to understand the opportunity. It is not yet a firm project but just an opportunity to advise the customer and earn some goodwill. (Managers sometimes do such pre-consultation with vendors in order to gather information which they can incorporate into their recommendations and get internal recognition.)

A multinational customer, with whom we had a close global relationship, was entering a new market and invited us to participate in their first project. Being the first one, even the fragrance choice came from the customer's headquarters and we were asked to supply in the local market. Everyone in the chain assumed that cost was a decided issue and that the local subsidiary was fully aware of it, as the product selection was done at its headquarters. No one from our company posed a question on the costing. A few weeks before delivery of the first consignment, the local purchase representative was shocked to know the cost of the fragrance. The customer's response was to cancel that fragrance and re-issue the brief that opened it up to other competitors as well. We still won the business but could easily have blown it. When in doubt (even when not in doubt!), it is a good practice to ask and get specific responses to key variables of your product or service.

The reciprocal norm is also true. It is a good practice to declare your terms and conditions to the customers. I would assume this is always done. However, variations that are negotiated in many follow-up discussions may be left uncommunicated in writing. This could lead to convenient 'assumptions' by the customer, which could return to haunt you. Account managers are sometimes guilty of this, especially as they go through the closing motions excitedly, unless there is a legal vetting step in the process. Some companies use a checklist at some stage in the buying process to ensure that customer's actual responses are captured in writing, to serve as a permanent record. Wherever account manager's opinion or assumption is reported, it should be clearly marked as such.

I would strongly recommend that companies whose account management process are still in developmental stage draw up a checklist of questions to cover key usage, product and commercial information that can elicit broad outcomes and the most relevant information. The checklist ensures that there is uniformity in the company. This is also a critical area to train account teams as the natural style for many adults is to assume and talk rather than ask and listen.

4.4   SKILL UP TO CUSTOMIZE THE STORY, THE APPROACH AND THE DELIVERY

Does storytelling form a key tactic in your engagement with customers not just in the beginning but throughout the relationship? Does your company have a well-crafted story to tell customers? How do you skill up your account team to adapt the script to specific situations of customers?

Customers in B2B domains are alike and yet different. More importantly, key customers expect individualized treatment. Companies, however, cluster them into segments based on various parameters applicable to their industry and try to over-standardize customer-facing activities and pitches. So there is a need to strike a balance between individual and group approach. While strategies, approaches and underlying data deck maybe similar within a segment, the uniqueness of each customer needs to be reflected in presentations, conversations and proposals. This is not just changing logos and names in the presentation deck. It means customizing the story in terms of key message, focus, emphasis, length, terminologies, sequence and the like. This is not just for the very first meeting but for all situations where there is a formal presentation (PowerPoint or no PowerPoint) to a group of people (small or large). Elevator pitch, as we refer to these days, is a capsule of such customized work. Why storytelling?

All sales pitches and presentations are in some ways storytelling occasions. It is the occasion to build emotions into your logical constructs that can establish human connections, leave lasting impressions and generate meaningful responses. The story has to be relevant to the customer, to her style of orientation, to her order of importance or immediate needs, to her required time duration and should have a beginning, a course and the end. Unlike a true or fictional story, it is preferable many times to begin with the end (what will the customer achieve if she buys your product or service or adopts your idea) and then play the logic of how you arrived at it. This helps in keeping the attention, especially if you have reasonably hit the nail in terms of identifying the issues to be tackled. One of my bosses used to compare it to a mystery novel with a difference—the crime is solved in the first page! Every time the customer nods during a presentation or meeting, you could count one agreement point.

Advantages of Storytelling

Jennifer Aaker, a marketing professor at Stanford Graduate School of Business, had each of her students give a one-minute pitch. Only one in ten students used a story within his or her pitch while the others stuck to more traditional pitch elements, such as facts and figures. The professor then asked the class to write down everything they remembered about each pitch: 5% of students cited a statistic, but a whopping 63% remembered the story.

'Research shows our brains are not hard-wired to understand logic or retain facts for very long. Our brains are wired to understand and retain stories', Aaker says. 'A story is a journey that moves the listener, and when the listener goes on that journey they feel different and the result is persuasion and sometimes action.'[2]

Sales conversations can thus be organized to be stories at a fundamental level of understanding. But there is a big difference between the two. The most significant advantages offered by storytelling (with adequate preparation) as opposed to an extempore conversation are the fact that the thoughts are better organized and the delivery is multi-sensory (audio, visual, tactile, etc.). It is the difference between watching a movie and listening to a lecture in a lecture theater. It also promotes a better two-way dialogue which is what we want in customer meetings. Further, storytelling sharpens our ability to present simple facts with emotions. Repeated practice helps us to internalize the contents. Storytelling, if done well, can also communicate a good brand value about your company.

In order to be 'accurate' in tailoring the story, account managers need to fill the company with as much customer-oriented information as possible and as accurately as possible. This could potentially include product range of customers, their competitive positions, recent performance trends, likely pain points, likely audience to a presentation or discussion, responsibilities and profiles of the person (young intern, long time VP, dashing marketing guy, frustrated technical head, cynical purchase manager, etc.), their relative roles and importance, language expected (formal or informal, talk or two-way conversation), likely customer questions, buying criteria, possible outcomes from the meeting and so on. Armed with this, we would write a presentation and even a script, at least for the first five or ten minutes, to get a smooth and impactful start. I am not referring to presentation techniques

---

[2] Brianne Carlon Rush, *Science of storytelling: Why and how to use in your marketing* (theguardian.com, August 2014).

alone, which I am sure readers would have honed already, but building the right storyline, the right content, the right tone, the right emphasis and the right amount of formality can be an arduous task. It is a classic 'show and tell' occasion and demands your best dramatic and narrative skills. Depending on how fluent you get to, you could build embellishments like rhetorical questions and role-plays with colleagues. The focus, however, remains on 'delivering the message' in an interesting and retainable way.

Ideally, this should be practiced in every discussion and not just the first major presentation. The variety of interests that your customer's departments have means that your story may have to be told in different ways, with different angularities, to appeal to these interests. Scripts and focus may be different, but the core message remains the same. The advantages are the same, besides the fact that you may encounter new people at every presentation. To get the right overall package, we also took care of the balance between visual and text and other best practices of presentations. Audiences retain sounds, images, emotions and people interactions better than words and tables in the PowerPoint slides. Similarly, allegories, brand imageries and others convey critical messages more crisply. It is certainly important to present coherently, your 'core message' of the presentation, but perhaps even more important is the manner. The message may be lost in a badly conveyed story.

In a recent project where I was the coach to a group of university students who were tasked with recommending new marketing strategies, the students put up pictures of an 'older' unexciting actress and a younger, mass-followed actress to convey the new brand image change they were suggesting. The pictures said it all.

We trained the account managers repeatedly to bring this into their normal style. Many succeeded to the level we wanted them to. As with any storytelling situation, the importance of tones and emotions in right doses cannot be overemphasized. Storytelling may have cultural and regional characteristics to reckon with. Japanese culture, where meetings acquire serious and formal overtones, allows for less flamboyance, for instance. Nevertheless, the idea can easily be culture-fitted.

Customized storytelling was one among the many tools that got us valuable time with customers, especially since it was not the industry practice until that point of time. The fact that we were selling more often to marketing professionals provided a more appropriate fit for this strategy. Things, of course, can go off course sometimes. In one of our meetings with a leading multinational customer, the vice president of the division (a very senior manager) walked in suddenly to join the presentation. We sensed that he would be there for a short period and would want to listen to the essence of our story. We quickly zoomed into it, and to our welcome surprise, the discussion with the VP lasted half an hour and led to important projects subsequently. So having a plan B helps as well. Another simple tip that we practiced was: the hard copy of our presentations were given only at the end, in order to ensure that everyone focuses on what we were saying. I am not sure how this plays out in different cultures, but most customers in Asia did not mind it. The most irritating thing is when the audience is flipping different pages to your stage of presentation. If reading through some pages was the objective, why should there be a speaker in the first place?

In some businesses like ours, it helps further to provide a tactile experience to the ideas rather than just the words and pictures. We would very often make mock-ups of products, including packaging designs, to give a more holistic form to the concepts proposed. Taking the software example again, I recently was in the audience when a vendor presented a school management software. He was reasonably prepared and wanted to show us a demo of the system. The main thing missing was he had not done a simple customization of some of the screenshots and was pedaling a standard demo. Our team bombarded him with questions and he had to reschedule the meeting where he would show a customized version. The software vendor did not lose the opportunity forever, but in normal circumstances, a second chance may not be offered.

New Technologies Are Making This Easier

Video technologies (amateur and professional) and film-making techniques have made such presentations or stories more vibrant, close to real-life (or fantasized, if you want it), sleek, funny and memorable. Virtual tours, enacted testimonials, visual cues to abstract ideas or three-dimensional views, virtual reality (VR) and augmented reality (AR) modes are more powerful tools than a bland listing of bullet points. In today's PowerPoint presentations, the length of written script is less and even the spoken words are partially replaced by visuals and videos. Every idea can be represented graphically or through a film and this has greatly enhanced the power of impressing customers. Companies who have had a long experience with storytelling must now embrace these new tools to get a step ahead. Start-ups with better 'show and tell' mindset are now offering services for companies to outsource their video needs (just as the older generation managers outsourced copywriting for marketing collaterals). Don't ignore the fact that the age of the new managers on the customers' side is bound to fall every time. With new managers on the customer's side, enter new generation thinking and digi-tools in customer interactions.

There is another subtle area of caution. When you present something proactively or in a storytelling context, the tendency is not to reach a definitive conclusion or plan further. For all the work and resources put in, it is vital to seek some follow-up agenda based on the presentation. It could be as simple as a further meeting to discuss one of the ideas, sampling for trials, a sequel brainstorming or a conversation among a smaller group of people to delve deeper into one or more shortlisted ideas. The follow-up agenda has to be agreed in the meeting, with timelines and people. There is no free lunch, we may remind ourselves. Customization has to find a home where it should be possible to monetize it. Customers are let off the hook if this is not done and the presentation will just be a piece of enjoyable history. Account teams are sometimes guilty of not converting the opportunity of a good initial conversation or presentation. Some treat it only as a goodwill earner, but that is not enough remuneration for the effort. The stories are tools and not orders. We do want to win the war, not just battles. Account managers in our organization were trained to seek migration to the next logical step in these meetings and get some agreements with customers.

Get Ready for Your Own Story

The following steps could be used as a preparatory guideline to exploit the storytelling tool (see Fig. 4.1):

(i) Build a core content consisting of your sales message, unique competencies, compelling value offered and a clear enunciation of customer benefits. (Care should be taken not to overload the presentation with preamble, company details, etc.)

(ii) Use precise language and articulate with key terms.

(iii) Transform the content into a vibrant presentation deck using all possible (and relevant) modern tools (audio, video, etc.) and techniques outlined above. This is key to the whole idea. (Outsource this if your in-house talents are limited for this.)

(iv) To help account teams to 'plug and play' (to a major extent), develop four or five different versions of the core presentation, as applicable to different types of customers (based on size or sector or stage of evolution). The number of 'variations' depends on the number of scenarios in each industry.

(v) Prepare concomitant aids like samples, concept boards, mockups and touch-and-feel objects.
(vi) Generate translated versions into local languages, where critical (Spanish, Chinese, Indonesian Bahasa).
(vii) Train account managers in delivery of the presentation in the storytelling format (some companies ask specialists like marketing managers or pre-sales personnel to present to customers).
(viii) Provide feedback to the account managers (or other managers) on improvements, time management, theatrical moments, dramatics, emphasis points and so on.
(ix) Some companies add teasers from these decks on to the websites, customer forums or other online engagement platforms.
(x) Presentation decks can also be for sub-topics like pricing and mapping decision journeys if these constitute large chunks in the customer engagement.
(xi) Shorter version of the main decks is another useful preparation to be used as elevator pitches where contact time is expected to be short (C-level meetings, for example).
(xii) Update the decks periodically (once a year at the minimum).

Now, how does your story look or read?

Fig. 4.1 The story design

4.5   COMMUNICATE PROMPTLY, CLEARLY AND COMPLETELY

> Does your account team practice high-quality professional communication internally and externally? Do you have processes to ensure that communication is prompt and comprehensive? What are the organizational rules and norms of internal and external communication?

If I had to choose carefully an order of presenting the dos, this would rank up there. A vital piece of strong account management practice is communication. Though it is fundamental to any business and great strides have been made in the past few decades to theorize the subject, consistent, prompt and professional communication can still be elusive for many companies. The account management routines in these companies either underplay the importance or have a poor understanding of the standards required.

One of the companies with whom I worked on an assignment had the practice of bringing key customers to their headquarters periodically. The objective was sound in that such visits contribute positively to several areas such as goodwill, new perspectives, building new relationships, exposure to the larger capabilities and linkages to supporting managers. However, all this can be meaningfully achieved only if the communication is right—communication with the customer and with internal managers who will be the hosts for such visits. Account managers in this company were generally 'stingy' with communication. In one case, the account manager wrote to his contact at the headquarters that the 'agenda will be as usual'. It was so vague. The counterparts had to ask several specific questions to clarify the objective of the visit, the areas of general and immediate interest for the customer, the people who need to be present in the interaction, the mix of social and business time, specific takeaways that the customer may expect and so on. Such comprehensive information was not a routine practice with account managers in that company.

Areas to Excel

Communication with customers has to excel in three areas: *precision, comprehensiveness* and *promptness*. To this, one could add linguistic polish but in non-native countries, this may be difficult to aim for. We will take up comprehensiveness first.

In majority of B2B interactions, each discussion with customers tends to cover many topics and projects. Whether you are writing to specify the agenda for a meeting or writing back the minutes after the meeting, every single issue needs mention. Issues that are less important to you may be more important to the customer. Therefore, it is not a good idea to focus only on what is at the top of your mind. Each issue should cover the subject briefly and round off with the next steps and by whom and by when. Without a follow-up phrase, the writing is incomplete. 'The customer also invited new ideas for their y brand' is not a complete record of the discussion. How does your company intend to respond to that, by when and who will be responsible for that activity?

It is extremely important to practice precision in language. Choice of words, phrasing of the sentence, clarity in call to action and brevity are key components of precision. Thus, 'the customer did not appreciate our proposals' is not as precise and useful as 'the customer felt that our proposals are too bold considering their brand's conservative positioning'. Readers who were not in the meeting could draw different meanings depending upon the extent to which the language is precise. This is even more imperative while writing to customers, as ambiguity or contra suggestions are to be completely avoided. 'We will rework our pricing' is different from 'We take note that you have requested for better pricing. While it appears difficult, we will explore all options'. If you were the reader, what different things do these mean to you? Take time to draft customer communication. If feasible, run it by another person. It is even advised to rest on it for a day before punching the 'send' button. Language tends to improve over time and with more reading and thinking.

Account managers can be lazy when it comes to making written visit reports, either to the customer or internally. The advent of SMS and e-mail on the go may have aggravated this, as many reckon that jotting a couple of points in one or two words via these media is sufficient. This is a dangerous habit. In our company, there was a rule that a 'visit report' for each customer visit was to be prepared and sent to relevant internal people within 48 hours. It had to be comprehensive and precise as well. They had to make that time. It was a discussion item during annual performance appraisals. Some companies follow templates (most CRM software can do the same) for such reports to provide prompts to the writer. This is fine, but the content has to be generated by the account manager. Similarly, any communication that needs to go to a customer, after a meeting, had to go within three–four days (this was to provide time to check facts or to include deadlines for promised items or to secure management clearance). Copying relevant people (internally and at customers' end) is also critical. Carelessness in this can cost you friends or even sales opportunities.

Oral and Written Communication

What is the role of oral communication in account management? It is often limited to routine matters (other than formal presentations or meetings) and confined to presenting arguments, courtesies, personal topics or interests, matters of deliberate choice (sometimes necessary for confidentiality) and routine matters. I would imagine that substantive business communication would be in writing. The balance between oral and written communication is one of the key aspects to determine. Too much of oral communication takes away the formality and contractual nature of discussions or decisions and becomes difficult to enforce. The extent of care in written communication is difficult to practice in oral communication, which is often extempore and maybe casual. This could lead to misunderstanding, assumptions, unintended commitments or incomplete messaging. We had a rule that any commitment on commercial issues had to be followed up with written confirmation. This applied to customer's commitments as well (orders, prices, deliveries and other terms). Account managers change and so do managers on customers' side. The only way to preserve discussions and agreements for posterity is to record them. Verbal 'reports' do not supplant this. In the name of 'busy schedule', many account managers neglect this fundamental rule. Companies may also tolerate it, especially with experienced account managers, who may have longstanding customer relationships. Sales leaders tend to be lenient on this as well. In some countries like Singapore, it is an accepted norm for anything constituting an agreement between two parties (even between me and my university) is a written exchange of letters, signed by both parties. It is usually the starting point and a 'necessary' gateway condition for further steps.

Examples for Refining Communication
Some simple examples of how language precision can convey very different things to a reader are given below in Table 4.1:

Extending the narration slightly to remove ambiguity, including next steps, using clarifying language, being specific with the details, frank assessment of prospects and so on, helps to enhance the value of the

Table 4.1 Communication refinement examples

Item	Version 1	Version 2
Decision on buy	No decision has been taken yet	Decision is pending final drawings to be submitted by us within two weeks
Trials	Customer will conduct trials in February, with our product	Customer will conduct performance trial in standard operating conditions, for one week, with our products and record data
Expected orders	In the next few months, orders will be lower	Orders will be at 80% of standard rate for the next three months and will go back to 100% gradually
Product training	To conduct product training in May 2014	We have to conduct product specification and usage training for commercial department (about 40 people) for 2–3 days in the last week of May 2014 at customer's office
Pricing	To revise pricing as per customer's request	To review pricing and revise downward, if justified. To communicate in 10 days. Customer's expectation is 2% lower from next quarter
Competition	A new vendor has approached the customer	A new vendor XXX Corp. Has given initial presentation to the purchasing and R&D last month. The presentation was well received. They may be included in the next round of briefs. Customer is non-committal about it now.
Change of personnel	A new VP marketing has taken charge	Ms. Nicole Schwab has taken charge as VP marketing from 1 Oct. she comes from ZZZ where she was brand director for 3 years. We had a courtesy call with her. We need a follow-up visit in 3 weeks

communication, especially for a large number of other people inside your organization, who perhaps were not part of the customer meeting. Account managers need training in skills and attitude orientation to embrace this 'comprehensive' style of communication. Companies with low tolerance for deviations will reap the benefit.

If your system is less than robust, it is a good time to make a start by defining expectations, rules, guidelines on language, responsibilities and consequences for non-compliance. It is also a good idea to provide templates and examples in your context for easy adoption. It is a great challenge to rein this in if no standards have been prevailing for a long time. If you reckon that you have a good existing system, it may be a good idea to audit the actual communication vis-à-vis standards and provide feedback. Including communication as an aspect of evaluation in performance appraisals has a positive driver effect as well.

4.6   Prepare a Good Comprehensive Account Plan

If you don't know where you are going, any road will get you there—Lewis Carroll (1865).

What is the foundational basis of your account management activities? How does the support team inside your organization know the areas and time when their involvement is needed in an account? Do your account managers share their strategies and actions with the rest of the team? How can you measure the effectiveness of your account teams vis-à-vis expectations?

The fundamental tool for achieving success with accounts is the preparation of a solid account plan. An account plan is different from the marketing or the sales plans. The unit of focus in an account plan is the 'account' or a customer. There are several templates and ways to prepare one. However, they all have to contain some key elements. A plan has to be prepared for every account. In our situation, we even prepared separate plans for different categories or divisions of a customer as these acted more or less as independent customers and the customer teams could possibly be different. In the IT industry, this could take the form of a plan for each application area like sales, inventory, HR, production and supply chain. In the context of a medical equipment company, it would be useful to prepare separate plans for the different disciplines of a hospital—cardiology, pulmonology, orthopedics, nephrology, ENT and so on. The technology maturity of these departments may be different and there may be a totally different team in each of these, besides differences in the size of the opportunity or the price of individual products.

Plan Essentials

In a research paper covering a study of 78 international companies, Lynette Ryals and Beth Rogers of the Cranfield School of Management, the UK, conclude that 'across the four phases, some common defects were identified. Where key account managers had relied on only internal data, or numerical data, without checking with the customer, the plan was on weak foundations. These characteristics were usually found alongside little or no analysis. Even with good analysis, confusion between strategy and action was common. Strategies were also confused with outcomes and the plan was confused with a budget. Strategies might appear only as possibilities, or without inputs and outputs. They might not be prioritized, or assessed for risk. Questions may be raised which were not answered, or options presented with no preferred choice. Some plans seemed to consist of distilled optimism in which all strategies succeeded and all accounts grew'.[3] These are indications of how a plan could be poorly written.

The plan should start with the vision and mission for the customer— yes, much like how you would strategize for your company. The account team's vision is a good evidence of the clarity with which the customer and his importance to your company is viewed. Vision statements like 'to be the top supplier for the customer' or 'to secure at least 50% share of the wallet' are significant postures that would enable the plan to be built on well-thought premises. The account manager (or the head of sales or the CEO depending upon your company) needs to envision the future relationship with a customer and articulate it in terms of measurable endpoint. This has further advantages, as the whole support team will be able to perceive and understand the vision. Needless to say, the vision needs to be realistic.

---

[3] Lynette Ryals and Beth Rogers, *Key Account Planning: Benefits, Barriers and Best Practice* (*Journal of Strategic Management*, Vol. 15, Nos. 2–3, May 2007), 209–222.

A good plan also has the 'current' situation as a starting point. What is your current level of business, contacts, relationship, conversations, efforts and results? Your future targets could be independent of the current outcome (especially if you are ambitious), but your roadmap to achieve those goals will depend a lot on your current status. The next step is to frame the goals or objectives, ideally quantified and expressed in SMART terms (specific, measurable, achievable, realistic, time-bound). (See Fig. 4.2 for a suggested framework.)

Hard Goals
We often find that managers are not trained to articulate goals in the 'hard' sense. They would rather say vague terms like 'improve business' or 'get a good share' or 'maintain good customer satisfaction'. None of these is measurable. A smart goal needs careful articulation. Some examples would be 'to attain a sales revenue run rate of $x per month by September' or 'reach 65% of customer's total annual purchases by December'. This is a hard commitment and therefore needs careful consideration and drafting. Personal goals have a similar analogy. You would want to 'lose five kilograms in six months' and not generally 'lose some weight'. The goals become actionable

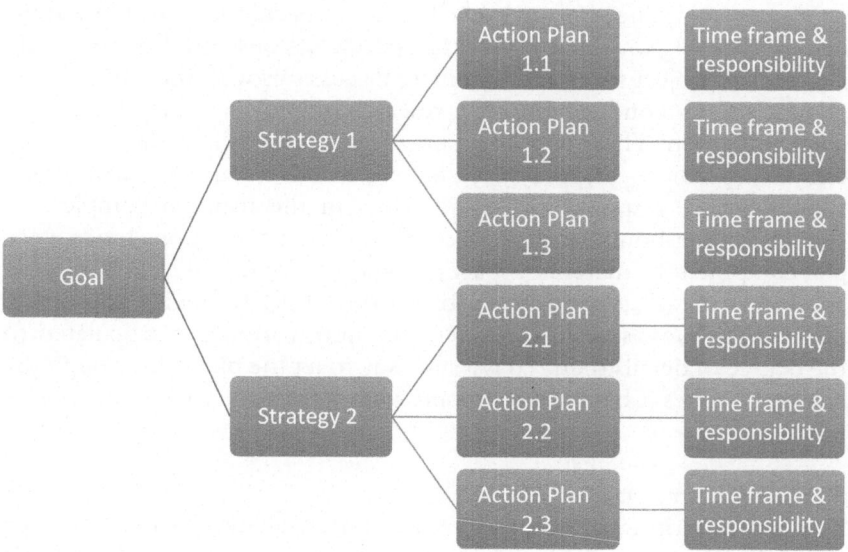

Fig. 4.2   Account plan framework

only if the SMART features are identified. In some situations, you may also have intermediate goals which are a prerequisite to being able to achieve the final goal. For example, if you need to capture x% of the customer's wallet, you may wish to include a sub-goal of capturing y% of the largest division, which maybe a necessary condition to be able to achieve the fuller x%. We normally encourage having not more than three or four key goals per customer to be realistic and manageable.

The next task in the plan is even more intellectually demanding. Each objective is then mapped into a few strategies—for example, to obtain a specific revenue target, one strategy could be to focus on certain brands or to focus on certain categories or to focus only on new launches or to work on replacement opportunities. There may be more than one alternate or concurrent strategy to achieve a goal.

Strategies, by definition, are broad 'road maps' and are not specific actions. If you want to double your revenue (turnover) in two years, one strategy could be 'acquisition'. Some people mistake strategies for actions or for goals. There is plenty of management literature enunciating the differences and the ways to use them appropriately. In a nutshell, goals refer to the 'what' and strategies to the 'how'. Most people understand this at the semantic level but mix them up while writing a plan.

The strategies need to be backed up with specific actions. For a strategy of 'focusing on category A', the specific actions could be to initiate an internal project for brand Y, initiate discussions with the customer on relaunch plans, conduct consumer research to understand the brand specifics and so on. These actions assume legs to run only if three parameters are specified—responsibility, timeline and resources. Each action should be the responsibility of someone in the team to complete, it should be time-bound and resources required for the action (funds, people, equipment or materials, space) should be delineated clearly. A good account plan will synergistically blend the goals, strategies and action plans in the most seamless manner. Any information not articulated to the degree of details required is a sure way to let the plan fall through the cracks. It makes it harder to pinpoint what went wrong when the goal is not achieved.

Writing the Account Plan
The task of writing the plan therefore is painstaking and needs a close oversight. Our plans were written and re-written based on review by not just the supervisor but also the supporting cast. If a responsibility was

assigned to a supporting team member, that member had to accept the plan. The summation of all goals for an account manager should add up to at least the sales target for the customer for the ensuing period. Some goals in the plan went beyond the standard one-year cycle. This is important to reckon as well, as some B2B buying cycles stretch beyond 12 months. The author of the plans was always the account manager even though he or she would draw help from other members of the team. This ensured that there is complete ownership of the plan. Some companies also include a signing off step of the plan by the owner and the approver. Account managers need training to prepare high-quality account plans. It is quite likely that you have salespeople for whom conceptualization or clarity are not strong suits. Instead of providing 'assistance', it is more advisable to train them up to the task as it is a major part of their commitment.

A top-down sales budget or a bottom-up sales target without the rigor of account plans is an empty goal or at best a wish or hope. Failure to achieve it cannot be analyzed and the next cycle would be the same with the same results.

Reviewing Plans

Plans are firm but not always cast in stone. Subsequent developments do create conditions for plan reviews. It is good to schedule a review at least once during the plan period. The review is also a good opportunity to remind everyone of the goals originally set, especially the ones which have gone on hiatus. The review would also help in rebalancing efforts and resources if new opportunities have emerged. The end-term review of the plans (usually at the conclusion of the plan period) should include an achievement versus plan map for each of the goals. This review rigor will ensure that the account plan stays as a living document, guiding all account management activities in the company.

Famous contemporary author Alan Lakein said, 'Failing to plan is planning to fail'. He is absolutely right.

Sample Template of Account Plan (Refer Table 4.2)

Account name: Barney & Rich.
Period: July 2016 to June 2018.
Prepared by: Neil Armstrong, Account Director.

Table 4.2   A sample account plan

Objectives/goals	Strategies	Action plans	Responsibility	Timeline	Resources
1.0 increase sales from 1 million to 2.5 million in 24 months	1.1 new launches 1.2 replacement of existing portfolios	1.1.1 participate in all new launch projects 1.1.2 research and keep a palette of products ready. 1.2.1 selectively target existing products ready for change.	Neil Armstrong Linda Carter	Sept. 2016 Jan. 2017	3 FTE $15,000
2.0 secure an entry business of 0.25 million in haircare	2.1 propose new launch in the economy segment 2.2 special entry pricing	2.1.1 present market analysis to new brand team 2.1.2 develop and present two new concepts 2.2.1 formulate a special pricing strategy for the first 2 years	Neil Armstrong Kathy Wilkins Bob Drummond	November 2016 March 2017 March 2017	$12,000

This document should be preceded by the necessary 'fact sheets' and 'analyses'. It would be useful to link each objective to a goal of the customer so that there is perfect strategic alignment. For example, if your company's goal is to sell the next version of an inventory software that allows real-time monitoring of stocks and locations, you may want to add the customer's goal (or benefit) of saving on inventory carrying cost by x% over a period of y months post-implementation. Incorporating the customer angle and vocabulary in the plans is another step toward fulfilling the stakeholder objective.

Depending on the circumstances and intimacy with a customer, some parts of these account plans could be shared with the customer. We managed to do that with many key accounts. It can lead to a healthy dialogue on priorities and approaches (and an indirect declaration of our wishes). If the goals are congruent, there is a greater chance of achieving them. It also helps to enhance credibility and build trust, which are often the foundation for longevity of business, first right of strike in new opportunities and continuity of the relationship beyond people. A well-articulated account plan also builds confidence in customers of your strategic thinking ability, preparedness and resource commitments. This was another key differentiator for our company. Of course, account plan preparation is a good training tool for account managers to develop visioning, perspectives, detailing, goal setting and strategic thinking skills, all of which they need when they move up to bigger roles. Account plans are also good documents for transitioning an account responsibility from one manager to another.

CHAPTER 5

Proactive Relationship Management

5.1 APPROACH THE CUSTOMER AS AN EQUAL

What is the relative position your sales team is most comfortable with vis-à-vis your customers? Do your practices and tactics give undue authority and power to your customers, wittingly or unwittingly? Does your sales team believe that it is perfectly acceptable to assume a subservient role versus the customer?

Vendors and customers are not always equal. This is potentially a wrestling point between them. Salesmen need to develop the attitude and courage to want to be treated as equal to the customer—not in aspects like size but in professional competence, commercial capability and business commitment matters. This has to be earned by the salesman and the company. In most markets (especially in Asia), salesmen take a subservient position and may subconsciously dilute their convictions and arguments, as the customer is always considered 'right'. If the customer is a large company or monolithic organizations like the government departments, vendors suffer from a size complex which affects their professional behavior on the job. This results in weak negotiations, conceding unreasonable demands of customers or simply positioning the company at a disadvantage, not just for one transaction, but in the whole relationship. Equality in the relationship is an attitude to be developed and can take

© The Author(s) 2018
B. Shankar, *Nuanced Account Management*,
https://doi.org/10.1007/978-981-10-8363-1_5

time. The key is to build this aspect strongly into the sales culture and for senior sales supervisors or leaders of sales teams to act as role models while transacting with customers.

When my former company began operations in India, we were considered as rookies—competitors and customers had been around for a very long time. This did not deter us from exuding the right amount of confidence and assuredness to handle customer conversations. In many cases, our door openers came, in fact, through CEOs or heads of businesses. Interaction at that level is even more challenging. It was important for a late entrant to demonstrate that ability early in order to ward off the doubting 'Thomases'. In our experience, showing the right parity was often welcomed and seemed to give us the appropriate professional tag, far from the 'arrogant' tag that some feared we would get. B2B dealings are all about substance, objectivity, mutual respect and sincerity, and thus, there is little room for either party to seek power. This happens only when one of the parties yields to such an influence. Desire to be treated as equal does not tantamount to supplier being insensitive to the customer or being high-handed either. It's just about commanding your rightful seat on the table and ensuring that it is given.

One of the good examples when this plays out is in getting information from customers (especially deeper insights or facts not in the public domain). We found that customers tended to respond only to specific and well-directed questions and were reticent about sharing information suo motu. Information is power and some customers would imagine that they hold an upper hand (an unequal position) if information is not openly shared. Our sales team was initially too reluctant to ask frank questions, as it was feared that it may be considered impolite or intrusive. Readers may be familiar with this situation, especially if the conversation is between a junior salesperson and a senior member of the customer organization. Apart from training the sales teams to phrase the questions better, we prepared a question bank that would help in making sure a substantial amount of information is gathered every time a customer is met. This acted as a confidence tool to fight any natural diffidence. In our experience, customers learn to respect good questioning methods. However, as communication experts would advise, it's also the salesman's body language that may invite guarded or unfriendly response.

Will You Walk Away from Unequal Deals?

Equality can also be demonstrated in other situations, especially when you are faced with unreasonable terms from the customer. Sometimes, customers leave you with a Hobson's choice—a bad deal or a no deal. It is a good testing moment to see if your account team and your company can establish the equality that you desire.

Our strategy was, in a selective manner, to walk away from deals that we felt were not fair to us. Of course, we did this politely and often citing our reasons and even financial calculations where it involved pricing. This ensured respect for us and yet we made sure we didn't burn bridges.

The whole operation needs careful management, and once again, we fell back on training. Salesmen were presented with situations in training sessions and asked to pick a yes or no answer (relating to a customer scenario) and to justify their position. Over time, many salesmen became comfortable with saying 'no' to customers when they felt strongly about it. This is particularly harder for a company that does not have leadership or a strong position in the industry and is eager to gain market shares quickly. If these tenets are established early in the game, salesmen grow up to embrace them more strongly and build appropriate skills. We were tolerant toward loss of an order occasionally and generally backed the salesperson when he or she took a contraposition with the customer on price or deadline or other services when faced with an unreasonable demand. Establishing our rights with the customer was encouraged as long as valid justification was evident. Customers have rules of engagement and so should we. If the equality is practiced to a higher degree, you could potentially even get plus points with the customer. Ability to weave through the customer's organization effortlessly depends on achieving this professional parity, as we could demonstrate in many cases.

We know that a B2B customer could be a large organization with several layers and people. Thus, even if it is not the policy of the customer to treat a vendor unequally, it could be a result of behavioral dynamics between the salesperson and his or her primary contact. Salesmen can be guilty of fostering this as a means to get brownie points at that level. This needs to be discouraged as subservience is a long-term weed. It is sometimes a challenge in the Asian context to fully achieve this, as the unequal mindset is inherent in the psyche.

For the top 20% of your customers, you may like to draw up an 'equality index' table. The self-scoring ratings would be based on your assessment of routine interactions, behavior of the sales teams vis-à-vis the customers, enthusiasm with which your company is received by customers, your track record in winning tricky points in the buying cycle, your ability to secure desired prices, customer's keenness to invite you to more coveted opportunities, your ranking as a supplier and other soft factors like these. It may be a tough exercise in the beginning, but over time, you will come to terms with these qualitative assessments. Once you have the ratings, share it openly with the account teams and seek ideas for improving the ratings where you are doing badly (by your own standards or vis-à-vis competition). You will be surprised that many of your team members are not even conscious of this and may, in fact, offer many easy-to-implement solutions if there is a prima facie *psyche of establishing equality with customers.*

5.2   REVIEW CUSTOMER RELATIONSHIPS PERIODICALLY

Have you faced situations when customers defected suddenly? Is your sales team guilty of allowing a decline in customer relationships, noticed or unnoticed? Does your organization enthusiastically reward salesmen who bring new customers without adequately assessing or rewarding the ability to sustain and renew relationships? What processes do you follow that could alert you (or confirm to you) about adverse trends in every customer relationship?

Like all relationships, a reality check is absolutely necessary for customer engagements and must be done as frequently as feasible. The temperature of the ties between a vendor and a customer fluctuates over the long engagement. It reaches some very high points but what is more disconcerting is when it reaches the lows. It causes greater anguish if such temperature dips are not captured. These are the symptoms that perhaps everything is not going well.

In order to review a relationship, you need a reference point. This is the 'relationship' vision or the purpose. Your company should have started with defining the nature of relationship with a customer, the different elements, resources, enablers and contact parameters. 'For some reason, purpose-setting tends to evaporate when it comes to relationships. Just as there are many purposes that can make a company great, there are many kinds of effective relationship models. In both cases, it's the CEO's job to form a vision for which direction to take, and embed that vision within the organization.'[1] While the purpose of any customer relationship is to enable a flourishing partnership on a sustainable basis, the contours can be different in different contexts.

Factors Contributing To Relationship Strains
Let us look at factors that can contribute to gradual loss of bonhomie between a supplier and a customer in a B2B setting:

- *one or two soured deals,*
- *changes in personnel on both sides,*
- *customer's change of priorities or focus that escapes supplier's attention,*
- *changes in customers' value chain that impact your product or service*
- *stepped-up effort by one or more competitors,*
- *lackluster performance of customer's brands or businesses where you are associated with*
- *global realignments of companies, suppliers,*
- *change of terms by one of the parties,*
- *changes in customer's organization that alter the power equation or decision dynamics,*
- *changes in influences or voices,*
- *mergers, acquisitions,*
- *declining financial performance of either party,*
- *service slippages (especially recurrent ones),*
- *perceived lack of transparency (or other trust-deficit factors),*
- *mishandling of a crisis (or a near crisis),*
- *infrequent meetings when there is no deal on the table,*
- *customer paranoia that they have become less important in your scheme of things,*
- *perception issues about your company or your account team,*
- *perceived loss of privileged relationship (like the other woman syndrome),*
- *surge in competitive activities (especially new nimble competition),*
- *salesman's unacceptable behavior,*
- *shifts in customer engagement models that the supplier is slow to embrace,*
- *erosion in the perception of win-win equations,*
- *new organizational chemistry which supplier fails to notice and the list can go on.*

---

[1] Charlie Brown, *Too many executives are missing the most important part of* CRM (*Harvard Business Review*, 24 August 2016).

Customers do not like to suffer in 'silence'. The only way they show their displeasure is by gradual retreat and a shift in loyalties.

There is no clear 'tipping point' when the customer is ready to defect. It is often a slow snowball, but signals are provided along the way. The person who can perceive the change first is the account manager. However, they are often the one to miss it too. No news is not always good news in such scenarios. Loss of intimacy is often unmeasurable. Account teams could be in denial for a very long time before business starts to get affected. What can solve this problem is a formal review between the customer and the supplier, perhaps once or twice a year depending on the business and the situation.

We also forget sometimes that what keeps relationships going is saying 'thank you' periodically. Remember that B2B customers are also emotional. Even if a rational reason seems to be responsible for the 'drift', beneath that may be an emotional complaint—of neglect, lack of gratitude, ungracious act, loss of informality, inflexibility and feeling of being taken for granted, among others. The review is a great opportunity to appreciate warmly the business that the customer has provided. Some companies use special occasions like Christmas or similar days of the local calendar to exchange gifts. While this is a good symbolic act, it has become cliché and everyone does this. A stronger show of joint commitment is necessary to keep teams motivated.

Formal Reviews

We instituted a system of annual review with major customers. The review was formally notified, invitees identified and agenda agreed upon. The agenda could also include some irritant issues (often pricing, deliveries, perceived competence) as it would not be complete without listening to any woes, which can be the trigger for the start of decline if not detected and addressed. It took us a few reviews to get the tone and content of the meeting right, but the results were there to see. Many of our customers became longstanding loyalists, with several ongoing projects and ongoing sales.

One example stood out. Wipro consumer care, the consumer arm of the global IT giant, became our customer in our early days of the operations in India and stayed as our customer for over 20 years, through multiple product launches and relaunches and through several change of operating and senior personnel on both sides. During the period, the business grew several-fold for both companies, reaching to about ten times the original size.

In addition to the regular reviews, we organized a formal five-year summit meeting where CEOs of the two companies participated in some sessions, held at retreat venues. We used the opportunity to redefine expectations, identify new plans and, in some ways, renew the vows, as it were. It was also an opportunity for many members of the team from both sides to participate and share.

Some of these customer reviews lasted a whole day and included lunch. Some others even had short training sessions for the customer teams in our industry or product understanding, including how to write a good brief to a supplier. We benefitted from it but so did our competitors too! But we treated it as the best investment you could make to revitalize long-standing customer relationships without the overhang of mundane thorny issues. The atmosphere provided for a constructive approach and not the standard supplier-customer standoffs that are common. Both parties, in some sense, would use the moment to 'forgive' for mistakes and move on. Depending on how frank the discussions went, we even had customers volunteering feedback for improvement of our services, products and ideas for some new initiatives. It takes two matured parties to conduct a review of this nature. Therefore, the concept needs to be canvassed and sold properly in order not to become ritualistic. The culmination of all these was a collaborative and co-creating spirit and a good platform for business continuity with our key customers.

It is ironic that we often have weekly, monthly, quarterly and annual reviews for all internal functions, but there is usually no structured review with the most important stakeholder, the customer. Even small shareholders have a chance at the annual general meetings (which must be held every year in most legal systems) to be heard.

We also believed that involving both the teams was a good gesture of getting to know all the people and easing buy-in from all quarters. Like in the west, some deals in Asia are also struck in other places like golf courses or yachts, but for our teams, a professional review was the norm. Written minutes and a working agenda, with timelines and responsibilities, followed up these reviews. So it didn't have just the social and camaraderie color.

Agreeing on Expectations Is Important

Some customers are unsure of what to expect in such reviews, especially when it is held for the first time. How much introspection and deep discussions should they expect? What will be the takeaway for them? Selling organizations need to lay the ground clearly, set the agenda and ensure that the customer has an equal role in the review. Customers would be hesitant to be a party to a unilateral tone to the meetings or may walk in with lurking suspicions of where these would lead to. Educating customers is an integral part of account management. In some cases, even the concept of account management and the benefits to the supplier and the customer may have to be explained thoroughly to incentivize the customer to join hands. Customers may have been bitten many times by one-sided arrangements that they were blindsided to engage in.

It is relevant to draw parallel to the B2C world here. Companies now have a systematic way of soliciting user satisfaction levels through formal surveys. Banks and telecom companies do this with specific periodicity (once or twice a year) and track changes over time. In the B2B context, this has now become the new tool for measuring vendor performance. In the technology industries, customers rate the vendors on various parameters and provide overall and segmental scores. These surveys are often administered by third parties to promote frankness and remove bias. While it does provide a reality check, it may be too late to discover dissatisfaction through a survey and hence this method is at best a lagging evidence rather than a leading alert.

You need to be able to catch the first signs of thaw. Besides, when you can get face-to-face feedback, any other source is of secondary value. We are not interested in mere statistics that surveys can throw (e.g. 78% of customers are happy with the communication regarding launch of a new product line) but would like to deep-dive to the root causes of concerns that can potentially manifest in worse outcomes. A standard questionnaire adopted for surveys can also be self-limiting and lack sufficient customization. A new B2B customer, for instance, may have very different issues and assessment yardsticks compared to a longstanding one. Surveys would also be seen as less 'intimate' in the context of the stakeholdership aim we seek. If your customer base consists of a large number of small and medium enterprises, surveys may be a more practical option, but not otherwise.

As an aside, the concept of our annual or five-year reviews/summits was later extended to our purchasing side as well. We gathered our suppliers (including competing suppliers) at our cost and discussed plans and issues and secured their commitments. Contrary to early fears, suppliers were happy to participate in this and rub shoulders with their fiercest competitors. The pre-ordinate goal of these meetings remained as sharing of plans and securing mutually agreeable commitments rather than smart commercial negotiations. Such a gathering inspired many suppliers to seek further meetings with us. With measures like this, our company managed to reduce material costs by up to 25% in some cases, standardize qualities and streamline supplier choices. We also received feedback from the suppliers that these annual meetings helped them in their goal setting process and even in their investment planning. In countries where we held these meetings with suppliers, we were the pioneers of this practice in our industry.

Companies who are new to the idea of periodic customer reviews could start with a handful of key customers in the first year in order to gain experience in the modus operandi. It won't be long before you step it up to include all key customers, as the benefits will be overwhelming. The gradual process will also enable you to fine-tune the 'flavor' of the reviews to your and your industry's needs.

5.3   EXPOSE YOUR LARGER ORGANIZATION TO CUSTOMERS

Do you often face the dilemma of how much of your organization your customer should meet and get to know? Or do you have account managers who are possessive about their relationships and want to own them solely? Does your larger organization feel that they are working in the dark without having adequate exposure to customers? How do you ensure that your organizational strength is appropriately leveraged and showcased?

In B2B sales, we meet several managers and departments of our customers. How much of our organization gets exposure to the customer and under what circumstances? Companies often do not have a well-articulated strategy on this and maybe doing this on a 'need' or 'ad-hoc' basis, both of which have no rules. There are several advantages in taking a liberal position on allowing wider people-to-people interactions on a planned basis.

'According to Learning International (Corcoran, Petersen, Baitch, and Barrett 1995), customers like team selling because they feel their concerns are better heard and their needs better met. Learning International also points out advantages to sales organizations in that team selling selects team members based on expertise, allows multiple inputs into strategy decisions, and establishes a relationship between companies rather than just between a salesperson and the customer.'[2]

Our attitude was simple. In addition to the generous information sharing idea propounded earlier (Sect. 3.6), we decided to expose more members of our organization to the customer. Which of our managers or executives went to see customers depended on circumstances (but more often than not), but many had the opportunity. This is not the norm in most organizations. The norm is for companies to deal almost exclusively through the account manager and a supervisor (also a salesperson). The rest of the organization learns about the events and conversations through their ocular. There are several limitations in this tactic. Besides, it could actually be a potential advantage otherwise. Quite unsurprisingly, it was highly welcomed by our customers when our technical, quality control, market research, purchasing and even accounting managers met customers from time to time, usually with the account manager being present.

As you can imagine, this had a huge positive impact on the morale of our managers and, more importantly, established a more transparent engagement with the customer. This was our definition of a 'customer-centric' organization. Our quality control head would even present a seminar to customer executives to help align our processes. Our application team discussed common issues while dealing with different chemical processes or ingredients and their impact on the fragrances. Our creative team ran 'olfactive' workshops for our customers to familiarize them with the language, odor interpretation and correct smelling routines. Many of these were calendared events, which ensured that there was a sense of anticipation from both sides for such meetings and that they are planned and executed well. Most customers were pleased with meeting the larger organization as it helped them understand the functional competencies and professionalism levels of the rest of our organization. Our reputation was enhanced with the professionalism shown by the supporting managers. How this impacted the purchase decision may not have been clear, but these contributed to the invisible votes in our favor when the crunch came. As buyers look for professional compatibility, strategic fit and other 'loosely' defined parameters for organization to organization engagement, a wider exposure is vital. This cannot be achieved only by marketing claims about the supporting competencies of the vendor organization (customers in B2B have come to regard mere claims as untrue until proven).

---

[2] Thomas N. Ingram, *Relationship selling: Moving from rhetoric to reality* (*Mid-American Journal of Business*, Vol. II, No. 1, Spring 1996), 5–14.

Do You Want to Shield Your Managers? Why?

Some companies go to lengths doing the opposite. They try to shield the supporting managers in order, perhaps, to keep their internal operations opaque (in the name of preserving trade secrets) or due to lack of confidence in their managers' ability to interact meaningfully. We did not feel handicapped in doing this, even if some managers did not have sufficient exposure to meeting customers. An unintended benefit was that some of the internal managers applied to become account managers, once they developed comfort with this process and this opened up the pool of applicants.

We also extended this belief vertically. Our global CEO would meet key customers once in a few years and we tried to seek meeting at the C levels. Similarly, other senior members of our company would regularly visit key customers along with the account manager. These are not just social gatherings or dinners but business meetings with a capsule approach to business stock-take, forward plan for ideas and the like. Such interactions did leave some follow-up action and not just business cards. The advantage of a customer meeting and knowing several key people in your company is unquantifiable, if managed the correct way. If there are reasons to believe that customer meetings are reported back with some bias, a diversified contact base would ensure that there is a balanced view of the course of the discussions.

Leverage Organizational Muscle

We believed in the concept that the 'organizational muscle', which is important for long-term supremacy with customers, gets built with each interaction the different experts have with customers. It is a learning opportunity for all and cannot be substituted by working in the shadows. There is sometimes an argument that this could be both expensive and time ineffective. I think it is an overstatement of the problem and can easily be managed. Video conferences and VOIP modes like skype are efficient alternative solutions.

Companies do have the practice of presenting teams in several industries. However, these are usually restricted to their assessment of 'need' in the meetings. Thus, in a software conversation, there may be a team consisting of pre-sales and product specialist managers along with the account manager. If this can be extended to project managers, costing managers, application developers, solution architects, product design specialists and many others (all of these people work in the background) and opportunities for their interfacing with customers is built into the contact process, the benefits can be enormous. These managers may help to configure the application more accurately and in some instances may even co-create new or extended applications, thus opening new doors and enhancing revenue prospects.

Communication is the key tool for effective customization of products and solutions and it is not feasible for the account manager to complete the whole circle or be able to translate all of the customer language and needs to internal departments. A number of software applications suffer from 'repair' compulsions due to lack of communication and clarity in the design phase. That could be a function of inadequate participation of 'design' or other support managers in the client contact process. In today's world of non-travel meetings and discussions, this is even more feasible without the huge costs involved in travel.

A banker client once told me that a principle that worked for his team was 'bring the customer into the bank and the bank into the customer'. The essence of this is to create a seamless interface between the bank and the corporate customer, through multiple contacts and activities covering the different functional representatives of the bank and the customer.

The participation of the wider organization, however, needs to be a planned and well-orchestrated one, directed by the account manager. Communication with customers (especially written) must be overseen by the account manager in order not to cause confusion with overall client management tactics or lead to miscommunication (or worse, unintended commitments).

5.4   Bond with Users, Not Just Decision-Makers

Are the users and the decision-makers (or influencers) different in your line of business? Does your account team cultivate a meaningful relationship with the actual users? Do you have a mechanism to track interaction with users and their assessment of needs, responses to your products and services? Does your organization enjoy a good rating with the actual users?

In most companies, the buying department is different from the host of users across the organization. These users could also be located in different geographies. These users could be office staff, maintenance personnel, factory workers, middle-level managers, IT professionals or the like. An extended argument on customer relationships is for a company to reach out to the users in the customer organization and not just people who are involved in the buying process. For a long and solid relationship, vendors need the support of the users whose voice may not be heard directly. The actual users, in our case, were staff in the factories and in technical departments. In some cases, this also involved staff in third-party factory locations, as outsourcing was prevalent to some extent. One of my personal experiences is worth recalling for many reasons.

A large customer's flagship brand was fragranced by our company for a number of years. They used to make their trial batches at a third-party factory. This factory was located near the landing zone of flights into Mumbai airport. We could only secure a trial during the night shift as the day shift was assigned for regular runs. As this was one of our major plant trials in the early days of our India operations, a creative perfumer and I decided to be available at the factory, just to have the comfort that all processing conditions were adhered to. The run took place from 10 p.m. to about two in the morning with some breaks. During the breaks, we both would catch a wink on two coir-beds that were in the compound, in the company of music from plane engines that were landing every few minutes. If I remember right, we got four or five batches made, made some quick assessment of samples and took them for further evaluation the next morning. The production supervisor at the plant was very appreciative of our presence and took some tips from my colleague to get a perfect batch run. (In this case, we of course had a vested interest to ensure that our product came through the trials positively.) It was a manifestation of how we thought about customer actions as an extension of our activities. In most cases, this was welcomed. It was, of course, always carried out with all necessary official clearances from the customer.

Unnoticed Experts

The lowest worker or officer in an organization is many times an expert in his activity and may also have a lot of information that may be useful to the seller. They may also possess unique insights based on their experiences in their daily jobs. They are often genuinely keen to share the information and, equally, to educate themselves.

Let us see how this argument bears out in another industry. In the software scenario, this aspect is even more critical. An ERP or any other companywide application has multiple users across businesses and geographies. Clients usually involve some 'champions' from the user base to reflect the user expectations more accurately. This has a limited purpose and only at the stage of design or rollout. However, the post-rollout phase is equally critical. This is when the real users are left to fish on their own. The standard training and hand-holding is often insufficient as users lurch from one issue to another. Software vendors taper their engagement slowly as the modules go officially 'live' and users wet their feet. However, they still need the expert support of both the internal champions and the vendor, which makes or breaks the successful introduction. Due to their disengagement, vendors lose the contact with the actual users and this could potentially result in both unfulfilled benefits as well as reputational hazards.

Customer Satisfaction at User Level

The thought that the seller's responsibility is complete when contractual obligations are met is not conducive to measuring effective customer satisfaction or customer success. Some software companies do measure post-implementation satisfaction among users. This could partially address the issue, but it is not a mandatory industry-wide practice. The day is not far off when some part of the contractual payments is linked to such satisfaction study outcomes. This would perhaps raise the stature of this important requirement in customer engagement.

Whether it is a product or a service industry, blue and white collar users' pulse is critical to track on a continuous basis. As part of the account plan, we embedded factory visits and visits to technical centers (these were often located in smaller unglamorous towns and took arduous travel modes and several hours to reach) into the account manager's agenda. From the grapevine, we gathered that our competitors were not doing as much of this. These visits were used to foster relationships at that level and in many cases useful information was gathered which otherwise was not available. The visits on the rare occasions helped to negate adverse 'feelings' that built up due to lack of awareness or knowledge of our products or processes.

Ask your account managers to prepare a list of all users or user groups and draw up a contact plan post installation or post implementation (post sale) of your solution. The interactions must be tracked and feedback, complaint, praise or suggestion should be sought and recorded. If this is a new practice in your company, start with the top 5–10% of your accounts and extend to the others after ironing out the process. Keep recording other useful information gathered from the interaction with the users.

5.5   ENSURE THAT TRUST DEFICIT DOES NOT OCCUR

What trust-building measures do you routinely practice? Have you experienced circumstances that have led to a breakdown of trust or placed you in a downward trust spiral? Is your account team responsible (even partially) for the turn of events? Do you have a mechanism to detect loss (temporary or permanent) of trust and to address it?

Trust is the cornerstone of an account relationship. Its strength or fragility depends upon actions from both sides. We can only control one side of it. There are several triggers for trust deficit to develop. Many times, it is a creeping development and maybe unnoticed for some time. A customer's trust is a function of the account manager's trustworthiness and the actions of the organization, in a particular instance or over a period of time.

'Customer trust is a fragile thing. It is easily lost and can be difficult to regain. People have short memories and are somewhat inclined to forgive, but don't count on it. Clearly, the best antidote for a scandal is not to have one. That requires vigilance, involved management that asks a lot of questions, strong and well-understood organizational values and the unimpeded upward flow of information no matter how unflattering.'[3]

There is a long list of potential areas for trust deficit:

1. *Breach of confidentiality (or even alleged breach)*
2. *Any act seen as 'unfair' by the customer and not defended well by the vendor*

---

[3] Lawrence A. Crosby, Dean of Marketing for the Spears School of Business at Oklahoma State University, *The cost of customer trust violations* (American Marketing Association, 14 November 2016).

3. *Breach of competitive mandates*
4. *Prolonged neglect of the key managers*
5. *Pricing confusion (lack of clarity leading to impression of short-change) or a perception of overcharging*
6. *Serious gap between promised and achieved benefits not rectified*
7. *Political maneuvers of account manager, seen as negative tactics*
8. *Frequent service or delivery slippages*
9. *Communication gaps (or lack of communication) that lead to misinterpretations*
10. *Poorly handled transition of account manager(s)*
11. *Loss of public trust in the company*
12. *Violations of mutually agreed conditions, including informal agreements*
13. *Acts that may seem to amount to 'taking sides'*
14. *An outright fraudulent act by account manager or his company*
15. *Lack of (or perceived lack of) transparency*
16. *Lack of support to customer during difficult times*

It may be observed that trust is a delicate feature of account relationship and there is a plethora of opportunities for a deficit to slip in. The quantum of deficit is immaterial. It's a binary phenomenon.

One of the prime areas for trust gap is the handling of confidential information. This may be a well-understood concept in the western world. In Asian countries, account managers can peddle information from one to another, more as a tactical ploy rather than to harm any customer. However, this can boomerang badly in several ways and may tantamount to a felony of the ties. The account manager's reliability and professional integrity are put in serious doubt. The more critical consequence of this is that customers could tempt such managers by asking for more and in their anxiety to 'please' the customer, the account manager is likely to cross the line.

The Last Man in the Line

Large companies, with layered hierarchies, are even more prone to the exposure as the last man in the line is generally off the radar. Their actions or statements may never be recorded but can hurt the company. There is no long-term gain in doing this but it can potentially cause a serious setback to individual and corporate reputation that may become impossible to set right.

As a supplier, we were privy to a lot of information about impending market activities of various customers, including new product launches, relaunches, new packaging, new image, disruptive market maneuvers and even planned advertising campaigns. All industry players were thus required to not just sign confidentiality agreements but observe it in full spirit. All information that we shared with customers about the industry or a narrow peer group of the customer was of generic nature and those available in public domain. We would add our insights to the basic information as a value-add.

The major multinational customers had a non-disclosure agreement and even stipulated that we did not share their account managers and, in some cases, even the whole support team. This also called for an effective 'Chinese wall' between teams to guard against information leaks. As organizations become more open and cybersecurity issues are still not out of debates, embedding processes that classify information and secure them internally is mandatory. It is equally critical to ensure that the account managers embrace the right confidentiality code as any breach can sound the death knell for the company vis-à-vis the account.

One of our sacrifices when faced with guarding a customer's trust is worth mentioning here. A large longstanding national customer often competed head-on with some multinational brands. Their strategy was to offer a strikingly similar product at a lower price. While the fragrances were always different, on one occasion, the customer demanded that we offer a fragrance that we had sold to his multinational competitor (this fact was known to them) previously. Even though our multinational customer delisted the fragrance from the purchase program, we declined the demand as per standard norms. After several rounds of discussions, we parted ways with the national customer, never to get him back again. Customer's trust is binary—you either have it or you don't. It is also obvious that organizations are only as trustworthy as the individuals representing them demonstrate.

As we saw in an earlier chapter, the signs of 'mistrust' are easy to tap but are often ignored by account teams. The customer may not spell it out. In many cases, the customer just drops the intensity of the engagement and may eventually withdraw fully. The advisory for handling disputes and trust deficit is the same—face them squarely and swiftly. Restoration will be harder and will take longer if the problem is allowed to simmer. Let the customer know that you are concerned and keen on correcting the course.

As an exercise, rate the trust level you have with your top customers on a scale of one to ten (ten being the highest trust level). This is a subjective assessment and should be carefully done, based on real evidences. Any rating that is less than seven needs some care and attention. A rating of four or below is a 'pretty serious' situation requiring urgent action. To get a more balanced scoring, this may be done by the account manager as well as by one or two other managers who interact with a customer regularly. In a matured engagement, customers could also participate in this trust rating exercise.

5.6   Don't Brush Aside Reputational Threats

Have you faced situations when your company's reputation or standing was called to question overtly or covertly? What is the sensitivity your account teams possess in order to pick up such signals? What are your practices for responding to such situations?

The long tenure of B2B relationship also brings with it, ups and downs. Customer managers may change and transport with them their own experiences. Equally, the environment and competition may change and bring results that can impact your company's relationships. One vital aspect of this could be suspicions on your company's reputation—business, financial, ethical, human resource and so on. Questions on reputation could spread like wildfire within a customer's organization, and before you realize, you may be either asked to defend your position or, worse, silently blacklisted or ignored for business opportunities. The nature of such questions makes it hard sometimes to justify with facts. They may be unseen but simmering in the background. Good companies detect these issues early and address them proactively and squarely, as the long-term damage of leaving it unaddressed could be devastating.

When we tried to re-energize a weak relationship with a major multinational company in their China operations, we encountered a hostile president who accused us of being a supplier to 'counterfeit' manufacturers who allegedly were making fake products that jeopardized the market for legally produced goods of the multinational company. We sought some information on the source of the accusation but did not get any. Instead of merely voicing our denial of any wrongdoing, we went a step further. We provided sales data per customer in our China operations for the previous three years and sent it under confidence to the president. Under normal circumstances this information would be highly classified, but we chose this option to unequivocally demonstrate our bona-fide operations and innocence. The full length of the information drawn directly from our internal records (which was evident) meant that the subject matter was closed instantly. To be sure, we sought and received a communication from the president that the company was satisfied with our stance. We suspected that this could have been the handiwork of a competitor. Such reputational attacks could be debilitating and need direct and swift actions, to be able to make progress in the relationship.

A question mark on your company's reputation could also be subtly raised and may brew for some time before it hits the roof. In one instance, one of our top customers told us, in a casual conversation, that they felt a difference in the quality of recent batches of our supplies. While they could not say this for sure, they articulated it nevertheless. We investigated and located the problem as contributed by substitution of a raw material due to its non-availability. Our quality control had assessed that the substitution did not alter the quality. We declared this information to the customer and even demonstrated how our internal inspectors assessed the two materials and the finished products. To reassure the customer, we offered to provide a copy of the 'recipe sheet' for safekeeping by the customer, just to assure them that it was not being played with. Recipe is the secret in the business and is the intellectual property. The customer never had to refer to it again for that product nor was there any other reputational question marks raised over a long relationship. Customers may sometimes feel that they are being shortchanged and may or may not articulate it openly. This is especially true when the customer does not have hard evidence, but circumstances point to such a possibility. Before the issue boomerangs, it is critical for the account manager to sense such 'feelings'.

Reputation Goes Beyond Direct Business

In the list of buyers' wants mentioned in Sect. 1.3, we talked about ethical expectations. Customers may even get annoyed if your company is alleged to flout principles of child labor, pollution, workplace safety, gender practices, racial issues, money laundering and the like. Activists and an aggressive media have carried the tales to public domains in recent years. Bad news sells! As these are not directly related to the business between the vendor and the customer, there may be a tendency to dismiss them as 'rumors' and not act to quell the damage. This is where the vendor could take a misguided approach.

Many cases of visa frauds (by companies), gender bias in promotions, business deals in violation of UN sanctions and so on have driven large global customers to audit their vendors' record more thoroughly before or during engagement. As responsible corporate conduct becomes a non-negotiable gradually, vendors need to actively manage their reputation and any threats to that.

My business associates in the banking industry often refer to 'slow death' of enterprise clients following several actions of the banks that may give rise to suspicion. When they are ignored (sometimes callously), they could snowball into a permanent breach of confidence and eventually to termination.

New threats to reputation may arise from the cyberworld. It is more common in consumer markets, but it takes only one disgruntled customer or even a competitor to bring your reputation to the streets with some direct or veiled accusations in social media. Companies in service industries are more vulnerable to this phenomenon. In many cases, customers may not even report it to you, they will just move on. As industries get more and more competitive, customers find it too expensive to manage a tense relationship with a reputation-stricken vendor as opposed to finding another. Arthur Anderson company, the top audit and consulting firm, collapsed in such a scenario in 2002. While their contribution to the Enron scandal was under investigation, clients started to move away.

Even if it may be true that the genesis of a threat to reputation may not necessarily occur in the sales function, it is necessary to sensitize account managers to these possibilities. Senior management, by their response to such attacks, should provide a model code of conduct for managers to follow. As is often said, reputation takes a long time to build and just a fleeting moment to disappear.

CHAPTER 6

Organizational and Human Resource Imperatives

6.1 Don't Neglect the 'Well-Being' of Your Account Managers

> What policies of your organization are conducive for account managers to feel empowered and motivated? Are your systems set up to track unspoken needs of the account teams? Are your account teams treated well by your customers?

In the B2B world, account managers are not just salesmen. They are the brand ambassadors and in many ways synonymous with the company. In fact, the only account management asset is represented by account managers. Their well-being is of paramount importance in ensuring that they put their best foot forward for sales opportunities and build your company's brand. Equally important is for the customers to hold account managers in high esteem and treat them respectfully. This is not just in the hands of the account managers themselves.

Besides the usual factors like salary, benefits, mobility opportunities and recognition, account managers have higher order needs which stem from their comprehensive role that combines commercial and entrepreneurial skills. The manner in which each company empowers its account managers and consciously projects the right image can play out in a number of ways.

© The Author(s) 2018
B. Shankar, *Nuanced Account Management*,
https://doi.org/10.1007/978-981-10-8363-1_6

Empower Account Managers

All employees facing a customer are representatives of the organization. There may be an internal hierarchy but each person is performing an assigned role in supporting the company's business with the customer. Therefore, the customer may or may not be interested to know the relative levels of various managers. The account manager is the face of the organization. A manager who is empowered to take a certain decision should be allowed to do so under all circumstances. The customer should be clear on whom to deal with for different issues. The integrity of your manager's authority should therefore be protected. Even if your protocol requires internal consultations or approval, the respective customer-facing manager should be the one communicating the decision, if he or she is assigned that role, despite the temptation for 'everyone' to communicate to customers.

'Nordstrom trains and trusts its employees to do the right thing, and empowers them to do so. Its employee handbook has only one rule: Use good judgement in all situations. Employee self-direction has become increasingly important' and 'frontline staff are often on their own when they face customers. Therefore, it is difficult for managers to closely monitor their behavior. Research has also linked high empowerment to high customer satisfaction.'[1] The context of these comments may be the 'services industry' but they echo in all sales processes.

B2B deals may take a long time to fructify. There are several back-and-forth discussions and correspondences on the same issue (usually on pricing, other terms). We ensured that every time there was an update on an issue, the oral or written communication was the responsibility of the same person.

This logic has several angles. The customer should be clear on whom to deal with. Further, the customer should respect that authority. If there are instances when higher authorities intervene and hijack the decision power, customers get encouraged to go higher. By playing out your internal convention in public, you may trip up the motivation of the concerned manager. He or she does not have to live in the fear that someone is looking over the shoulders all the time or that he or she is only a temporary holder of relevant authority. Managers can also be timid and tentative, if they know that they do not hold the right amount of authority. (As a buyer

---

[1] Jochen Wirtz, Patricia Chew and Christopher Lovelock, *Essentials of Services Marketing* (Pearson, 2nd edition), 339.

myself, I have been puzzled by salesmen declaring that they would refer the pricing issue to head office as soon as objections are raised.) As B2B transactions involve teams and hierarchy of people, managers may usurp others' authority unintentionally, if there is any hint of encouragement to do so. These are detrimental to the account manager's motivated frame of mind.

The price domain has to be handled delicately to ensure primacy to the account team. When we presented our top management to customers, our brief to them was not to get dragged into any discussion on prices or other commercial terms and to direct the question to the account manager. Some account managers may forfeit the right if their organization does not support this idea.

Keep Account Managers' Missteps Outside the Customer Discourse

It was also an accepted argument that individual manager's capabilities or their failings cannot be discussed with the customer. Even if the account manager is directly responsible for a mistake, he was never the fall guy in front of the customer. An account manager who loses face with a customer on one occasion will carry the cross eternally.

There are benefits of doing the opposite of a criticism in fact. HR experts advocate public praise and private censure. The rule fits smugly for the account manager too. It would do a lot of good to the account manager's morale if he or she receives public praise in front of the customer. This would also aid in a rise in esteem from a customer viewpoint. A well-regarded account manager has a greater chance of longer-term success with customers and that is your goal. The new fashion is to lean on customer surveys for rating of account managers, but companies forget that the way they treat their managers in public (in customer's presence) can influence these ratings. Customers could, in fact, use account managers' well-being (and empowerment) as a surrogate for progressive policies of the vendor. As this is a subtle association, it may never be disclosed.

Top sales talents are difficult to find. This is true in all industries and perhaps at all points of time. Account managers reach their optimum performance levels after a lot of experience, perseverance, coaching and learning. They could easily be lost if their unspoken emotional needs are not met. Their well-being is critical to the successful deployment of account management. Stability of trained and matured account managers is a great boon to an organization—this comes from nurturing their emotions wisely. The leader of the account team is often the first person who could sense the well-being or otherwise of his members. Therefore, he or she needs to be perceptive to this aspect as well.

In your future employee satisfaction review, include aspects in the questionnaire that seek information from account managers on their motivation, their empowerment, their operating freedom, respect received from seniors, respect enjoyed with customers, motivation to go the extra mile, grudges and so on. You will obviously need to follow up on low satisfaction areas.

6.2   Avoid the Easy Way Out in Hiring People

> What proportion of your account team has come from outside the industry? What is your philosophy on hiring account managers without prior experience in the industry? What is the career track that you offer for candidates joining your sales teams from outside the industry?

I am not sure if this would sound like an antithesis to the advice of HR experts. Majority of companies believe in drafting account managers from direct competitors and expect instant outcomes. I would strongly back a policy of hiring candidates with the best credentials—and prior experience within the industry is not necessarily one of them. It seems like an easy ploy when you hire someone with 'ready-to-apply' skills and, more temptingly, 'ready-to-transfer' client lists. This is largely followed by insurance companies and lately by private wealth bankers.

The approach for a B2B company needs a fundamental rethink. Account management is a potential game-changing competitive strategy for a company. To harvest that competitiveness fully, it may warrant your own grooming of people, practices and the package to be unique and difficult to copy. If your company is planning for the long haul (which is how it should be) and is willing to back it with good human resource budgets, hire and groom. It is better to groom in your company's ethos, character and style rather than import such values. It may not be the easier solution but has enduring advantages.

We were very clear that this would be our policy. All account managers were hired from outside the industry but came with strong education, valuable experiences and keen minds. Each one of them was extensively trained in our account management philosophy. We also sought to hire people with a desire to learn and improve. Fast forward 20 years later, most of them are working in various parts of the same company even today, many in leadership roles. A few were poached by competition and some have gone on to do other senior roles outside the industry, as is to be expected.

We were newcomers to the Indian market, and instead of the temptation of getting us on the road quickly with poached hires (the rest of the industry had existed for over 10–15 years), we chose the slightly longer start plan by adopting careful selection, induction and mentoring programs. Our selection process included filters based on type and quality of education (including institutions), a series of interviews which had a bias toward problem-solving and even an essay. The whole process was coined to fit into the image of the account manager that we wanted to present to the customers. Learning from previous experiences was more important than the mere experience in a certain product line itself. It was clearly worth the effort as the results and the career graphs of these men and women have since shown. 'You can't teach new tricks to an old dog' goes the saying. In the account management context, this is largely true.

Ready-Made Managers or HomeMade Stars?

Companies reckon that they are playing safe by importing ready-made managers. This belief is based on many assumptions—the manager operates well without a system, his productive start date is 'day one' and customer acceptance will be good. There is no empirical evidence that this delivers better results in the long run (or in the short run). It is true that the cost of training is high and gestation for raw employees to perform is longer, but that cost will be paid more handsomely when they become well-trained stars. A grafted manager is more prone to be overconfident of his or her abilities or bring in habits that you may not find acceptable.

The analogy of a football or a basketball team is sometimes quoted but is not correct here, as we are not seeking instant wins in a few games or in one season but enduring lifetime value from customers. Recruitment companies have a simplified lazy approach as they match people within the industry. This, however, does not do any good for your company. In rare cases, such imports work out well and realign themselves well to the new employer, but the chances are slim, as re-grafting is a delicate exercise. One of my bosses used a term, 'recycled salesman', to denote the much-hopped salesman. We also found that home-grown talents help increase retention rates. Once they embrace the philosophy and you can show clear career paths, they don't become rolling stones.

Companies seeking quick growth in a market often find themselves in this dilemma of having to choose between industry veterans and talented youngsters. Small and medium enterprises may find it easier to buy trained resource. If instant sales are your goal, the veteran may deliver for a while, but such salesmen may often impede strong account management adoption. They may think that the company is dependent on their experience (companies even acknowledge it) and will be law-breakers rather than law-makers, as the primordial goal is 'sales'. Some of them may even turn out to be the source of negative influence jeopardizing a company's effort to create a unique image and appeal.

In fact, some leading global FMCG companies follow this principle for many functional roles, not just account managers or sales teams. Their mid-career or senior-level recruitments are very few. Fundamental to their strategy is the belief that all managers must carry the organization's DNA.

Rate your salesmen on practice of various account management tools and specific holy grail practices of your company and compare the scores of home-grown managers and grafted managers. It will not be a surprise. This could be used as a developmental tool in employee appraisal exercises. The next time you need to hire new salesmen, avoid the temptation of tapping the competition but choose a smart talent from outside the industry (allied industries may be a first stop). To develop conviction, you may like to build this strategy slowly from 33% of such hires to 100% potentially. If you have two or more divisions, different strategies could be used in different divisions and the account management outcomes compared (to develop internal conviction).

6.3   Don't Place Overdependence on Any One Individual

What is your approach to talent continuity? Do you practice a viable plan to ensure perpetuity of customer relationships, one that is independent of the people involved? Does your company suffer, when some 'indispensable' salesmen leave? How good are your organization to organization ties?

People are a key component of an account management strategy. But no individual should matter more than the group, the organization and the system. In the past few decades, stories of hero salesmen have tended to color the narrative of what entails a successful account management approach. It may appear that some people carry out all the tasks with ease and with mechanical precision, but it overlooks the fact that there is a whole host of enabling systemic elements, resources and people that play a complementary if invisible role.

How can a company maximize the contribution of its high-performance account managers while managing continuity and intensity of customer relationships? As discussed earlier, B2B selling is a team effort. Therefore, as a first doctrine, it is prudent to present a team of people before the customer, from time to time, including representatives from support functions. It is often said in the B2B context that the first sale could conceivably occur from the heroics of one salesperson, but subsequent sales and long-term loyalty depends on the whole organization. Due to the long-term nature of the relationship, continuity of high performance vis-à-vis customers becomes a cardinal objective.

In the industrial fragrance industry, account managers were always playing musical chairs among the key competitors. I have no doubt that this is the case in many other businesses. This can lead to over-reliance on one individual to carry the relationship, and therefore disruptions occur when people change, even if these disruptions don't last long. The short handover period is often insufficient due to the deep nature of relationships. In order to ensure that discussions, folklore, important facts, issues, agreements, ideas and stories are captured in company archives, we also insisted on regular reporting of customer visits and all customer related documentation to be on paper (or on computer archives). CRM software has made this easier to achieve now. Salesmen are able to do this on the go as well via mobile devices, and there is no further excuse for avoiding this, quoting drudgery. In fact, the value of this cannot be overemphasized as we also experience changes in customer's organization as well. It is important to bring new managers up to speed and the correct historical version and milestones in the pipeline projects and in the overall relationship.

Personal Chemistry or Professional Chemistry?
Many companies strongly believe that one of the critical success factors of good account management is the personal 'chemistry' between the account manager and the purchaser. This is a very limiting argument. Like all salesmen, account managers do need the right personality to be engaged by their counterparts.

However, given the complexity and potential value of the B2B sale, the chemistry is only a baseline necessity and not sufficient in itself. The myth that some account managers achieve better results only because of their 'chemistry' undermines many effective account management steps that such people embrace as part of their second nature. Not acknowledging that sends wrong signals to the rest of the team. The notion can actually be modified to 'professional chemistry' rather than 'personal chemistry' in which the professional conduct and practices are the basis of the personal advantage derived by an account manager. The only personal quality, if at all, that fortifies the account manager's clout with a customer is his or her 'personal' trust. We have dealt with this in several places in the book.

Readers may have read about the company that announced a 'Porsche' car for the best salesman and had to withdraw the scheme, as it found that salesmen were so aggressively competing with each other that they were poaching customers from other salesmen within the company. The external competition was completely lost sight of.

The 'superman' salesman syndrome goes against these tenets. Organizations that continue to depend only on them have accepted their bare talent cupboard and that their account management processes are not contemporary. In the war for good talent, it is not possible to insure against departures and vacuum. However, it is possible to insure customer relationships through a carefully crafted team and organizational account management approach. We ensured that all our customer relationships were intact even when key members of the account management team moved on (which included my own move as well). That is a good reflection of being able to manage simultaneously star account managers and deeper and durable account relationships.

Insure Against Impact from Sudden Departures

It is equally imperative to penetrate the customer organization and establish multiple contact points rather than depend on one gatekeeper. Some salesmen do not go beyond the gatekeeper (or the prime contact person) and thus the dependency syndrome can be equally detrimental to the relationship. Whenever I heard that someone was successful as a salesman because of the golf-buddy relationship he had with the customer, I would worry about its downfall one day. In most cases, that happened eventually.

HR experts generally support this view. They also recommend other insurance policies like job rotation or customer rotation. Many B2B companies are wary of disturbing a longstanding customer-salesman relationship. This is often the beginning of the problem. The longer these relationships continue (without other team members in the frame), the greater are the risks.

We had a case where one account manager handled a large Boston-based customer, a global market leader in their business, for over ten years and toward the end, he was not creating any new opportunity but merely milking old products. His motivation to reinvent the relationship was minimal, as longstanding revenue streams assured his bonuses. A potential disaster awaited the company. Our local management was then convinced to change the manager. The result, after six months: 15% growth in revenue!

In Asian markets, such solo acts are also potential breeding ground for collusion with unscrupulous customers and for improper money transactions. The primacy for the organization has to be clearly spelled out at every opportunity. Like succession planning for key positions, companies need to plan for succession of account managers, after every three–seven years, depending upon the industry and the situation. The first person to resist this is often the account manager himself or herself.

I suggest two planning exercises for organizations which consider themselves vulnerable to people changes and loss of customer intimacy. One is to widen the contact pool beyond the direct account manager. Sales support, marketing and sales supervisors could be drafted as additional contact points, with clearly defined roles. Account managers may resent this, but they need to be brought around.

The second is a succession plan—for each account manager, at least one potential in-house person should be identified for replacement if the situation arises. As a long run plan, medium and large companies should carry a buffer of 5% in the account manager bench. The additional costs would easily be justified by the smooth transitions that can be achieved by people groomed and prepped up.

6.4   REWARD YOUR SALES TEAMS ON DIVERSIFIED METRICS

Do you offer incentives and bonuses to salesmen that are linked to sales achievement alone? Does your reward system breed unhealthy chase of one goal at the cost of others? How can you use the reward system to balance multiple goals of account management? How can you build an incentive system that encourages long-term results and team performance?

Rewarding salesmen is an unwritten rule that most companies follow. Salesmen are incentivized based on dollar sales achievements in the current year and that is the more common practice. In some cases, unit sales or sales margins (calculated at some predetermined rates) are used as surrogates, if the dollar sales revenues are subject to external influences like inflation and currency exchange rates. There are other minor variations to the 'sales' based formulae.

This is a double-edged sword in a B2B environment. While it could take care of the short-term sales goals, the challenge is to find a better fit for account management. As we discussed in some of the paragraphs earlier, most B2B selling is team-based. It is not chess or golf. It is akin to soccer or basketball, but with a difference. The goal is multiyear and not restricted to one championship year. We have also argued that long-term durable results are the primary goal of the organization. When it comes to the bottom line, overall customer profitability is more desirable to track rather than transactional profitability. There is also the phenomenon of efforts in one period paving the way for results in subsequent periods. Given all these peculiarities in the B2B scenario, incentives that are only linked to current period sales will work against these principles and reward people erroneously.

Hunters or Farmers or Both?

Companies tend to show a bias toward 'hunters' as opposed to 'farmers'. In the B2B business, it is equally important to win new businesses and to retain and grow existing ones. Leakage from the existing bucket is often the genesis of low or subdued sales growth. It is important to train account managers with skills to do both rather than merely brand them as hunters or farmers. To ensure this mindset builds up, our account plans unambiguously slotted in new win goals and business retention goals for all account managers. The skills required may be different, but over time, account managers could be trained to be bi-dexterous. With new online and big data tools available for demand (or enquiry) generation, the job of hunters is that much easier in many markets.

One of the other components to consider is how much of your sales is due to the brand/company 'pull' and how much is generated by the sales 'push' effort. In some situations, a company's technology or other proprietary strengths (or monopolistic market advantages) would draw customers and sales are clocked automatically. Even where there is competition, some companies may be seen to be clearly superior, and therefore they can expect a certain 'automatic' order flow. (GE, Siemens and Phillips enjoy such brand and technology power in the medical equipment industry and Microsoft in OS.) On the other hand, there would be companies whose brand power is weak or there is fierce competition among equals and most of the sales are engineered by sales team's efforts. In today's markets, the latter type probably makes up for 90%. It would be wise to consider a lower weightage or lower quantum of incentives where the pull factors are strong and to consider a more generous quotient where the push factors are seen to be dominant.

Modified Incentive Models

The topic has received a lot of academic interest too. 'Furthermore, because marketing thought is shifting from a product-centric to a customer-centric view, it is imperative that sales organizations adapt accordingly by viewing their sales force from a customer profitability standpoint and be able to forecast sales force profit potential. The importance of having a suitable metric for salesperson evaluation is further evident when managing salesperson churn, which is considered a major pain point for firms, especially in the B2B space.'[2]

We modified the incentive structures to include other controllable variables such as projects pipeline, value of business defended successfully, gross margin at customer line level and share of wallet from key customers. Appropriate weightages were assigned to these in addition to current period sales. If your company is similar to Boeing or Airbus, where orders are more important than even deliveries (even if deliveries are the ones you can book in the accounts and report to shareholders), such metrics could also be added. The purpose of 'incentive' is to drive sales team behavior toward what the company desires. The short-term 'billed' dollars approach falls short. Most companies take the easy way out instead of establishing a more balanced metric suite.

A variation to this is an interesting concept a friend in an engineering company once elaborated. In this company, the salesmen bonus is based on calculating reward at every customer level centered around company and customer parameters met or exceeded. This included ratings from customer satisfaction surveys and other parameters from customer's point

---

[2] V. Kumar, Sarang Sunder and Robert P. Leone, *Measuring and managing a sales person's future value to the firm* (*Journal of Marketing Research*, October 2014).

of view. Once calculated, this 'team bonus' is paid to the account manager and the other team members based on a pre-agreed formula of sharing. This is a fantastic evolution, although I am not sure if any major company has implemented it. It could result in perfect alignment of your goals and your customer's goals, besides rewarding teamwork.

We have seen the havoc played by Wall Street bankers' bonuses or stock options being linked to short-term gains for banks (from derivatives and other novel but risky products). Sales incentive based only on top line is very similar. Besides wrongfully rewarding salesmen who operate with a 'quick' sales attitude, the scheme discourages those who practice long-term sustainable account management principles. Our business was partly global and partly local in nature. When fragrances are adopted for global brands, sales flow to several countries and there may not be any notable contribution from a local team. Developing a comprehensive metric for rewards ensures that there is no windfall from such outsider efforts. This is an important aspect for many global businesses to take note of.

Diversifying the Metrics

Even where current dollar sale is one part of the formula, some companies use 'incremental sales' as the basis, in order to drive behavior toward 'new' sales rather than allowing salesmen to cool heels based on past year efforts (may even be the previous salesman's efforts). Recognizing pipeline activities also would encourage salesmen to go after major but multi-step sales opportunities. Group incentive is another way to link rewards to effort of each individual in the chain and therefore drive better teamwork. Incentives are golden opportunities to modify and direct team behavior and companies should build a plan meticulously and painstakingly. Much of our expansion in key markets came from directing efforts toward new wins (low business levels in these markets meant low retention needs) by account management processes as well as annual incentives. The argument that sales incentives should be simple and based on one or two easily trackable variables cannot be carried too far to justify oversimplified 'revenue' based metrics only. It could still be simple and easy to understand for sales teams.

Here is one basic incentive model that reflects a balanced spectrum of efforts and results:

Current period sales $: 50% weight
Current value of projects or opportunities which are at an advanced stage (say, 70%) : 25% weight

Average gross margin achieved over the budget: **15% weight**
Other metric specific to the industry: **10% weight**

This is a simplistic 'level-one' model of a diversified formula used only as an illustration. More complexity could be added based on measurability and data availability. Some companies twist the first measure (current period sales) to 'current period sales achieved as a percent of budget'. By adopting this, you declare that achieving the budget and exceeding it is your real goal and not merely clocking a certain dollar sales. This adjustment would also help companies whose sales are seasonal. The other nuance you can bring in is to split revenue targets into different products or categories. This is especially useful if you want the sales team to focus more on some categories and not all equally. By suitably 'weighting' the different categories, you can push efforts in the desired direction. Companies who have a rigorous budgeting process can easily link performance to sales budget. The fourth variable can be chosen based on industry specifics—for instance, you could introduce value of businesses 'lost' if your business trajectory is flat and protecting existing business is extremely critical. A company that has a strong pipeline of new products may add the metric of sales achieved with new products till they acquire sufficient traction.

Some banks operating in the corporate banking space almost fully use customers' metrics for rewarding relationship managers. This takes away the short-term profit mentality and with it questionable practices.

The concept of monetary rewards for sales teams has, however, been regularly questioned. Does that mean accountants, human resource professionals, legal support people and many other staff and support functions contribute less to the growth and profitability of organizations? I do not claim to have a simple answer. However, a good balance of monetary rewards and a culture of performance, duty, going the extra mile and organizational well-being have a greater chance of long-term survival and a motivational platform. Life does not run on KPIs (key performance indicators) alone!

If you are at the start of the game using just sales dollars as the reward measure, it is time to embrace other metrics relevant to your business. You must move the needle gradually after initial experiments are successful and well understood by sales teams. The transition should not affect the motivation and performance of the team but not moving on will keep your organization behind in terms of contemporary practices relating to account manager incentives.

6.5   EXPLOIT FULLY THE BENEFITS OF COACHING, TRAINING AND MENTORING

> How much time and effort go into coaching and training account managers in your company? What is the level of comprehensiveness of these efforts vis-à-vis skillsets required? How do you ensure relevance and effectiveness of the coaching/training program?

It would be naïve to argue that companies don't train their salesmen. Most medium and large organizations have a training routine for salesmen. Skilling them up to the planned tasks is the common goal. However, there are degrees of doing this and sometimes companies are guilty of merely doing some routines without taking sufficient care with the design of the programs or with measuring outcomes.

Broadly speaking, companies can deal with training and coaching at five levels (refer Fig. 6.1):

1. Product/service training
2. Selling skills training (including standard sales kits)
3. Account management orientation (base level, relationship management)
4. Higher order strategic and analytical orientation
5. Leadership and cross-functional orientation

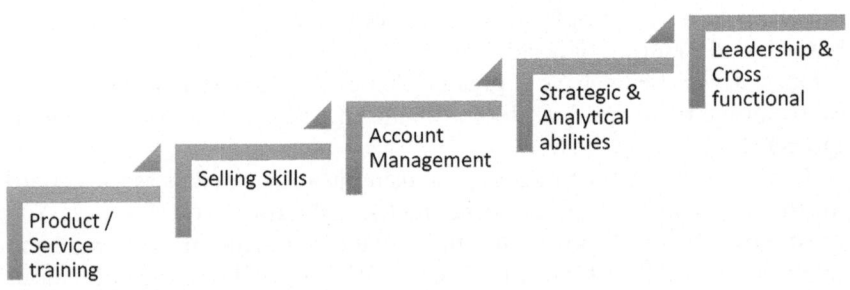

Fig. 6.1 Hierarchy of training

Some companies add other aspects like technology, sectoral knowledge and negotiation. It is very likely that many companies stop with steps '1' and '2' above.

Honing Skills Outside Educational Exposure

Selling and account management are not offered as professional degrees at universities. The classic salesman is a self-taught person who hones his skills on the job and by polishing his natural talents through experiences. He or she moves into sales responsibilities from different educational backgrounds and orientation. Some even cross over from other unrelated functions. Salesmen thus have their strengths and weaknesses. There are several aspects that can enhance or derail their effectiveness. For instance, when it comes to meeting people from different functions, some have comfort with purchasers (dealing at a transactional plane), others with technical staff (product development or engineering orientation) and some others with marketing group (brand knowledge, consumer insights, benefit analysis, etc.). A few people can pore over financial and corporate information. It is not common to find salespeople who are good at most of these or do not have pronounced weaknesses in any of these. It is thus a multi-dimensional skill matrix. To get that composite ability, salesmen need training, mentoring and exposure. With exposure to challenges, many can acquire these skills to a deployable and successful degree.

Account managers need different forms of training, coaching and mentoring in order to build in and cultivate the skills that are useful for a long journey. A one-off training approach will not help. Account management is a specialist skill and needs to be honed at different levels and to varying proportions. It is a process of indoctrination that shows results gradually. It is therefore suggested that training is staggered over time (instead of being frontloaded at the time of joining or taking over the responsibility) and even repeated from time to time. GE offers a lifelong training exposure in their in-house programs. Sales managers can sign up for appropriate level courses. The commercial leadership program is one of their flagship programs to groom sales and marketing leaders.

In addition to training in relevant sales skills, cross-training in adjacent competencies is inevitable to tune up to a comprehensive level. Thus sales teams may be trained to read balance sheets or in psychology topics like emotional intelligence, for instance. A well-run progressive training program is one that salesmen feel like coming back to from time to time.

Further, coaching and mentoring have to be used as complementary tools to conventional training. It is a well-known fact that on-the-job coaching has a larger (and perhaps easier) absorptive effect on the trainees. Adults' rate of learning and retention depend substantially on two things—immediate applicability and usefulness in achieving their goals. As situations differ and customer responses vary, account managers need a variety of skills to deal with these. More importantly, they need practice with using these skills. Coaching by a more experienced (and someone accomplished in higher-order account management approaches) is a surefire tool to make it a way of life. With video technologies becoming popular, companies employ the role-play technique to simulate customer conversations and salesman responses. Mentoring as a tool for education needs a larger commitment from the company.

Mentoring can have a positive impact on an organization, improving employee retention, engagement, and shaping culture. It can also serve a strategic purpose when linked to talent strategy, leadership development, workforce planning, and organizational goals. Mentoring programs, however, can quickly flounder if there is no buy in, insufficient structure, or lack of follow-through. HR and talent management professionals who want to establish successful and sustainable mentorship programs must ensure that the groundwork is thoroughly completed, that participants are trained, and that the program is regularly assessed for effectiveness. Mentors and mentees must have both the passion and skill to develop themselves as well as others to really multiply the returns on mentoring for the organization.[3]

Our annual sales conferences included two days of mandatory training for all account managers. Due to our mid-size, we were able to assemble them in one location within a whole region. There were two parts to the training. One was a reinforcement of basic concepts like questioning, potential analysis and standard sales arguments. The other part involved role-plays and case studies with customer scenarios. As much as possible, these were real stories taken from field experiences. In addition to the annual programs, it was very common to have junior account managers accompany senior managers or country heads to visit key customers to learn from the interaction. Such interactions provide valuable opportunities

[3] Horace McCormick Jr., University of North Carolina Kenan-Flagler Business School, Jenna Filipkowski, *How to build a successful mentoring program* (Human Capital Institute, October 2014).

to account managers that classroom training or coaching manuals cannot provide. Every such moment is a teaching-learning opportunity. On several occasions, we would use the long hours on the road from our meeting to the hotel or to the office to ask account managers to analyze our customer meetings and get them to draw lessons based on what they thought went right and what did not.

The introduction, agenda management in the meeting, tone of the discussions, phrasing of tricky comments, body language, questioning customers, listening, offering solutions, orchestration of the team present, closing comments, setting further agenda and so on are elements that cannot be fully learned in conventional training constructs. Coaching and mentoring through on-the-job exposures helps young people follow role models in language, relationship building, sales etiquettes and strategic account management. If these skills and behavior aspects can germinate early in one's career, they become second nature.

Common Training Practices Fall Short

Let us analyze some common practices. Too often, companies manage the whole process without care or a holistic approach that could leave them with a high proportion of average account managers. Together with the easy policy of hiring from competition (companies assume that this will reduce training and coaching needs, but that's debatable), development of top account managers is never going to be easy without a top training and coaching program. *There is never a fully sculpt account manager. He or she is always in the making.*

Organizations also face the problem of creeping bad habits of account managers. Sometimes, the more successful a salesperson is, the more likely that he or she leaves the 'conscious' practice to go to an 'unconscious' level and may not notice the change. Frequent training and re-training will address this problem. It is therefore a myth that experienced salesmen do not need training. They may not need training in rudimentary areas, but the gamut is large and the scope for slippage high. The buying-selling paradigm keeps evolving, underlining the need for refreshing skills, knowledge and attitudes.

Our experience also taught us that the coaching and mentoring responsibility has to be assumed by the leader of account management team and not delegated to the HR or training experts. They may tend to design umbrella or generic programs that are too clichéd and inapt, especially if the objective is to groom top quality account managers. While there is some merit in repeating some forms of training, mechanical administration of the same program with the same methodology does not challenge the fast learners or the high achievers. Companies thus cannot follow a one-size-fits-all philosophy. At our company, senior managers had training and coaching responsibility included as part of their KPIs and many turned out to be excellent coaches.

One question I have often been asked is whether an account manager is a naturally endowed person. I came from an accounting background and it wasn't onerous for me to embrace it when I moved to sales. There is a certain amount of rewiring of the brain but it can be achieved by effective training and coaching. In the same breath, it is possible for the conventional salesperson to be transformed to an account manager, provided the role change happens early in one's career.

Strange as it may sound, some companies, especially in developing markets, keep a lid on extensive training as they do not wish to train people only to lose them to competition. In markets that experience steep growth during some periods, the demand for trained people exceeds supply in many industries. This could lead to job-hopping within the industry. To curtail training for this reason is a clear case of shortsightedness. Having untrained or inadequately trained account managers represent your company cannot be more desirable than losing some managers to competition, most of which happens, in the normal course of all businesses, anyway. It would be a double whammy as lack of training opportunities, over time, will also lead to unattractiveness of a company for prospective employees. Further, as should be clear from the nuanced facets explored in the previous chapters, a good account manager without the supporting edifice of account management will have limited success. The manager and the system are non-separable.

Training the Supporting Cast Too

As must be evident, there is a large 'support cast' to the core accounts team and they need training and coaching too. Many of them end up in customer-facing situations. Once a manager is in that position, the customer does not differentiate between account managers and support managers. All are expected to perform to similar levels of professional caliber. There are potential dangers from inappropriate conduct or conversations or impulsive commitments. Planning tailored programs that seek to skill up the support cast is extremely important. This often escapes the attention of senior sales or business leaders. Similarly, if you are in an industry where channel partners are extensively used, the sales teams of channel partners need the same quality and depth of training and coaching. It is a grave mistake to assume (or devolve) that this is the lookout of the channel partner. The sales team represents your product or service to the customers even more than representing the channel partner's organization.

From my own experience, coaching has been one of my pleasurable tasks and a new skill learned on the job, whenever I had the role. Training others also offered me the opportunity to reflect on my practices, my strengths, weaknesses and tested my ability to stand the scrutiny of others. I am also convinced that my early opportunities in training and coaching while working in the corporate world skilled me up for my university teaching and project coaching roles that I took up successfully in later years.

Fortunately, in this area, companies can get a lot of help from experienced sales leaders, training organizations and consultants. However, customizing the program to your needs, your talents and stage of account management maturity is the leader's painstaking task. In a new account management setup, this could even take a substantial amount of the leader's time and energies.

CHAPTER 7

Customer Innovation Bias

7.1 ESTABLISH THE GROUND RULES FOR CUSTOMER RELEVANT INNOVATION

> What is your philosophy on aiding customer innovation pursuits? Do you have a rulebook for creating (or co-creating) customer relevant innovation? Does your account management team help to build an architecture of customer needs that can trigger innovation streams? How will you ensure that customers appreciate the value of your innovation support?

If there is one word that has dominated the corporate discourse in the past couple of decades, that would be 'innovation'. It has come to encompass anything *new, different or better*. Customers are constantly searching for lasting advantages in their products or services and innovation is their mantra to achieve this. Unfortunately, innovation is also harder to conceive in the normal course of business activities. It needs a certain mindset, processes and enabling incentives for an organization to achieve a perennial spiral of new things. In order to diversify the source of innovation, customers often turn to their suppliers. It is thus a great opportunity for suppliers to fortify their standing and relationships—provided they can meet the innovation challenge.

© The Author(s) 2018
B. Shankar, *Nuanced Account Management*,
https://doi.org/10.1007/978-981-10-8363-1_7

Companies not only established internal environments conducive to innovation but also began identifying, cultivating and taking advantage of a wide variety of external sources for innovation. Among such sources, suppliers are recognized as having especially large innovation potential because they know what the companies — that is, their customers — are doing and need and also because mechanisms for knowledge transfer from supplier to customer are typically in place.[1]

Innovation can impact or be derived from any of the following:

- Products or services (e.g. touchscreen phones, car services like Uber)
- Processes (e.g. ordering via e-commerce portals, just-in-time inventory, encrypted document signing)
- Usage (e.g. software as service rather than owned software)
- Technology (e.g. digital vs. analogue, online/digital vs. face-to-face)
- Pricing (e.g. bundled pricing vs unbundled pricing, telescopic pricing)
- Cost savings (e.g. fuel-efficient aircraft, new materials)
- Aesthetics (several consumer electronic products)

Innovation is of two further classifications—incremental or continuous innovation and disruptive innovation. A vendor could even realistically contribute to paradigm changes in the customer's business or product designs. Swedish packaging company Tetra Pak is well known for its customer relevant innovations, especially for the food industry. DreamCap™ 26 is their latest closure innovation, developed based on a consumer-centric approach to understand the drinking behaviors/habits and meet the needs of consumers while they are on-the-go.[2]

In order to embed a sustainable process for assisting in customer innovation, vendors need to conceive a robust program that consists of the following elements (refer Fig. 7.1):

1. Vision: What is your vision for the 'customer innovation thrust'—how much and in what areas are you keen to offer innovation to customers? The vision must encompass areas, extent, depth, customers who would benefit, how the innovation advice would be monetized (if at all) and how it would be communicated to customers.

---

[1] John W. Henke Jr. and Chun Zhang, *Increasing supplier-driven innovation* (*MIT Sloan Management Review*, Winter 2010).

[2] http://www.tetrapak.com/about/innovation, August 2017.

Fig. 7.1 Customer
innovation system

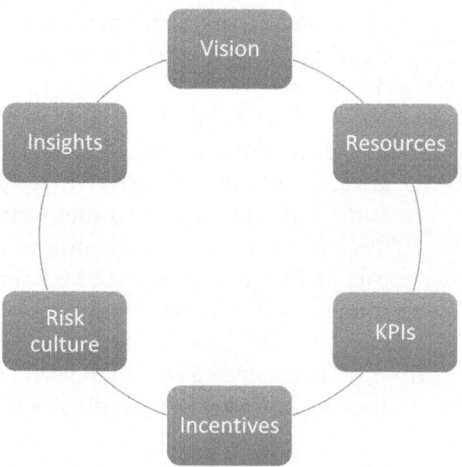

2. Resources: Efforts to find meaningful innovation will need resources in the form of manpower, technologies, marketing insights, space and so on. Half-hearted resource allocation will likely lead to insignificant or non-unique ideas. It may also dampen the enthusiasm of staff to join the innovation journey.

3. Encouragement: Incentives are part of this strategy. All staff involved in generating, testing and promoting the proposals must be driven by monetary and non-monetary incentives. These tasks will require special efforts and time allocation which need to be supported and rewarded.

4. Risk-taking: As customers look for novel ideas from vendors (that they themselves are unable to ideate), vendor's employees will need to cross the traditional risk boundaries. Avant-garde ideas are sometimes outside the standard circle of thinking. Customers will value ideas that are revolutionary, even if not fully tested or proven.

5. Develop insights in customer's business and markets: Each customer's domain is likely to be different in aspects like market segments, type of end-customers served, consumer behavior, pricing parameters, distribution and competition. Real ideas for improving customer's business will need powerful insights into all these areas. The two passenger aircraft companies, Boeing and Airbus, have an extensive understanding of the different segments, geographical markets, passenger preferences, competitive space in which airlines operate, costs,

prices and margins and maturity of the airline industry in the different markets. Armed with this, they are able to advise customers on fleet decisions.

6. KPIs: How many ideas to bring? If the innovation process works efficiently for a vendor, the question of how you set such goals will arise. How can you differentiate between the staff in terms of their contribution to the customer innovation strategy? You may want to use this to drive internal competition. The key performance indicators (KPIs) could be based on number of ideas that reach the customers or the monetary impact of such ideas.

In order to practice a very high level of innovation that sets vendors apart vis-à-vis other competitors, we discuss the following further strategies.

- Linking your product or service to the innovation ideas: An idea is worth its weight in gold if it can be incorporated into your product or service. That would guarantee continuing source of revenue from sales. Where possible, innovative ideas should therefore be embedded into your product or service. This would also make it less easy to mimic.
- Link up with external partners for expertise: It is conceivable that you do not possess all the expertise to pursue meaningful innovations that your customers would value. There is a great merit in identifying experts and drawing up alliances that could be a win-win situation. Many fragrance companies, for instance, team up with cosmetic ingredient companies to offer a package solution for skin care or body care needs. The synergistic advantage of two vital ingredients (some could be patented) offers an unbeatable combination.
- Use every opportunity to discuss innovation, not just everyday business: The real origins of new ideas are conversations. By indulging in freewheeling discussions with customers and decoding their pressing needs or unsolved problems, you get good hints on where to focus. That lands you a first-mover advantage with the initiatives. Vendors and their account managers should practice a culture of such discussions, as a routine.
- Set up customer group meets, conferences or forums to understand priorities: The other opportunity to set an innovation agenda is to assemble several customers into a conference that could discuss new benefits, new frontiers of technologies, regulatory changes, consumer shifts (of your customers) and next-generation products or

services, among others. If the discussions are well moderated, you could generate a powerful list of 'to do' things, which become the seeds for finding innovative ways or products.

- Fine-tune idea evaluation process: Every idea is not likely to succeed. Smart companies know when to stop ideas that are not likely to make the cut. There should be a periodic evaluation of the innovation projects at various resource points to check if further resources need to be invested and to make sure the end result will be interesting. This hard 'go' or 'no go' calls must be taken without fear or favor in order to get the ideas with the strongest legs to the finishing line. Companies are sometimes soft-footed and end up with too many projects that do not produce significant innovative ideas.

- Frame enabling sales rules: Assuming you have some really winning ideas on hand, how would you want to capitalize on them? Which customer or customers would get the first opportunity (right) and why? Are you aiming for direct revenue benefits from the innovation or a strategic position with your customer(s) using the innovation as the route? The right set of rules needs to be written based on the vision for the strategy.

A conscious strategy of lending active support in innovation and ideas to customers must be reinforced by a framework where all the above issues are deliberately addressed and systemic tools devised accordingly. If practiced randomly by one or two individuals or for one or two customers and on select occasions, this will not stand out as a competitive advantage that customers unequivocally associate your company with. Your competition could offer many clues as to how you would like to run the process that best suits your interests, priorities and resources, different from what the competition has to offer.

7.2   Create the Change Before It Happens

Do you promote an approach that brings proactive changes to your solutions or customers' products? How do you ensure that the account teams instigate proactive changes without discomfort? What are the principles behind vendor-induced changes?

Every company should work hard to obsolete its product line ... before competitors do. —Philip Kotler, legendary pioneer of marketing concepts.

We know that cheese moves. The question of 'who moves it' has been brilliantly dealt with by Spencer Johnson in his popular book.[3] In relations with customers, there comes a point when status quo is not good, either for the vendor or for the customer. It may not be good for many reasons and these stem from commercial outcomes of customers, competitive responses, changing market conditions and technology advances. For example, if you have supplied a clutch of servers to an organization maybe 12 months ago, would you take the initiative to propose a 'cloud' solution to the customer that negates the need for the servers? You probably will not. What happens if one of your competitors presents a compelling case to the customer, offers cloud solutions with the carrot of financial savings and buyback of the servers that you helped your customer install only recently? Isn't this a cheese moving moment? Would you want to respond to it after it has happened or make the moment yourself?

Account managers are afraid of disturbing what appears to be a smooth sailing phase. There are three lurking dangers—the smooth sail may be a waning perception and not real, it could be challenged by a competitor without any announcement or it could drive customer's restlessness, unnoticed. It is often like the tranquil phase of marriage, too quiet for comfort!

In the fragrance company situation, at every customer meeting, we would briefly review brand performances, the ones that we were associated with (to make sure the news was positive) and the other brands that we were not part of (to look for opportunities). If our competitors did the same (let us assume they did), they could find the chinks that they can exploit. In fact, we chanced upon some new opportunities by asking questions about competitors' products and being told of gaps. It is, therefore, important to ask the question 'how is my product or application or service doing?' every now and then. If you sense a 'less than' enthusiastic response, you should probe further, identify the issue and address it. This is similar to the advice of identifying and dealing with objections in the run-up to a sale. To do this with 'genuineness', account managers need skills to ask the right questions and need to be prepared with homework to offer either 'ready' solutions (if such solutions are available) or agree to come back with a solution.

---

[3] Spencer Johnson, *Who Moved My Cheese* (Penguin Random House, 2000).

The worst outcome of a question of the kind mentioned above could be that the customer is 'extremely dissatisfied' with your product or service and was only waiting to be asked. This shows failure of account management. If the account manager had done all the other things mentioned in this book—monitoring performance, maintaining conversation with users, keeping tabs on competition and so on—it would not come to this pass.

Thus, one of the principles of good account management is to instigate renewal or replacement of your product or service yourself. Initiate the change. This could be done in the form of commissioning a study of current performance or showing early prototypes of what could come next or dig into user opinions or canvass green field ideas that could lead to further concrete prototypes. In some sectors, issues can be identified by targeted user surveys (software applications, for example). The willingness to do this systematically could potentially sway the customer from noiseless attacks by a competitor.

General Electric (GE), one of the largest suppliers of aircraft engines, plans ahead for its new generation products, often creating the change proactively. 'The GE90 engine represents GE's continued investment in the future of wide-body aircraft. Combining the best proven technology from previous GE engine programs, NASA and military programs with advanced technology, the GE90 provides a highly reliable, fuel-efficient power plant for the Boeing 777 family. The Guinness Book of World Records recognized the engine as the 'World's Most Powerful Commercial Jet Engine'. Today the GE90 powers Boeing's 777 aircraft capable of flying farther, faster and more efficiently than their predecessors.'[4]

Keeping Competitors at Bay

You can improve the prospects of long-term loyalty from customers by being astute and systematic about this. The other advantage of being the change agent is to continue to keep competition away by being one step (or more) ahead. Many customers feel safe with vendors who can 'look after' the business even after it is won. This is akin to master health checkup of our bodies to detect any potential problems before they raise their ugly head. Some vitamins and supplements are necessary for vendor-customer relationships as well. Just as we have a program of continuous improvement in our internal processes or product designs, we need to do it for our products and services that our customers use. At appropriate points, we

[4] www.ge.com, August 2017.

need to bring in disruptive changes, before others can do it. This is not easy as account managers can be caught up in day-to-day issues and can neglect tasks that are more abstract or aimed at the future.

In industries where projects seem 'one-off', this can still be a valuable tool. A leading office design and furnishing company in Asia goes back to its more than 1000 clients every 18–24 months to update their interiors. That seems too soon for this field. However, they use the opportunity to hear the experience of the occupiers and bring in bite-sized affordable changes in areas like lighting, accessories, materials, artifacts, layout of open areas, curtains, electrical and customer interfacing spaces. Their objective is to keep improving the feel of the place, its character, functionality and aesthetics with step changes that not only evolve the offices but ensure that they don't fall behind in technology, new concepts or materials. This strategy also helps in ensuring that new managers and leaders are on-boarded without too much delay (this is usually a trigger for design change or overhaul in corporate offices) and that competitors with better ideas are kept at bay. As incremental investments are kept reasonable (and fitting the shoes of the customer), it is a win-win strategy for the two sides. The company eventually institutionalized this practice by developing 'upgrade packages' for different office concepts and sizes, so that the account teams actually have product solutions that could be offered readily.

Are You Ready to Phase Out Your Product?

In my college days, Sony was one of the great brands admired for its cutting-edge innovation in consumer products and being the first to market. One story that did the rounds (I could never verify it) was that when Sony's management signed off on a new product launch, it was done after verifying that the next version was 'ready' for the market! The company planned its own product obsolescence! Similarly, the policy of 'free' software upgrades by many companies is borne out of this idea. As new user needs emerge, how do you ensure that your product is not obsolete, especially in the technology space? Can you anticipate newer and extended applications of your product with minor upgrades that keep users loyal to your product? Many large technology companies often sign contracts with customers that guarantee lower prices from second or third year of the contract. How are they able to provide the reduction without sacrificing profits? One method is to re-engineer the solution using more updated system thinking and lower people and other costs. The guarantee thus forces the companies to embark on the renewal path suo motu.

Companies like Google and Facebook are engaged in doing this in the consumer space to extend the interest of hardcore users and to keep a constant pipeline of new usage experiences to counter user fatigue and new user demands that may surface. The B2B concept is similar and is many times explicitly demanded by customers.

How is this to be achieved? In our company, when we won a new business (or retained an existing business from a fresh challenge), we initiated a 'defense' project that sought to prepare us for the next round of renewal that the customer may plan. In some cases, we orchestrated such renewal proactively with the customer based on general tenure of the products in the marketplace. A defense project was as important as an 'attack' project (to secure new business) and received the same attention from all departments. Companies need to commission such 'renewal/replacement' initiatives with the goal of going back to the customer in a specified time frame with the next version of the product or service or application—with better performance and at lower costs (this, as you know, is every customer's dream).

Honeywell Inc., the world's leading company in industrial automation and control solutions, has instituted a 'Customer Advisory Board'.[5] The primary mission of the Board, as stated by the company, is 'to provide Honeywell Process Solutions with informed recommendations and advice on selected major strategic technology issues as well as to provide recommendations on feature enhancements'. This is killing two birds with one stone—being proactively ahead in the renewal cycle of products and technologies and soliciting customer endorsement early.

By leading or instigating change, you are signaling to your customers that you are more interested in their contemporary experience or benefits rather than your own desire to keep the sales meter ticking securely. Even if the renewal does not always lead to wholesale change of the solution but only a partial upgrade, it resets the life of the business. Whether the limited upgrades come at the cost to the customer is a matter of industry practice or subject to mutual commercial arrangements. But renewals always bring innovative changes with them. Customer happiness is important at all points of time, not just when you sold the product or service. This is built into the engagement in some cases where the assets sold are under the custody of the vendor (boilers, copiers, production equipment, software applications). The custodian is thus responsible for asset upkeep, asset

---

[5] www.honeywellprocess.com/en-US/about-us/Pages/customer-advisory-boards.aspx, August 2017.

upgrade, asset renewal or even replacement. The cost for this 'oversight' is built into the contracts. This makes it contractually imperative for the vendor to initiate renewals. Volunteering this benefit in non-contractual cases can keep you ahead in the race for customer's business.

Review all the major businesses that you have had for a certain period of time (one to five years, depending on the industry) and chalk out a plan to replace your product partially or fully, with appropriate innovation and contemporary functionalities. You should then plan a commercial strategy (upgrade pricing) to lead your customers to the newer versions, sooner than later.

7.3   Don't Be Afraid of Offering Bold Ideas or Initiatives to Customers

Does your sales team canvas bold ideas with customers? Do they have the skills (and belief) to convince customers to consider them and take them forward? Does your organization recognize and reward salesmen who have strong orientation to be bold and innovative?

This is the era of innovation and revolution—new product ideas, new technologies, new merchandising schemes, new ways of delivering value to customers, new paths to generate demand, new models of pricing and advertising, new service initiatives, new methods of doing customer surveys, new analytical tools, new customer engagement and loyalty programs and many other new things. Your customers are under pressure to reinvent themselves on a continuous basis, to keep ahead of their competition. How can you as an account manager help him or her? How can you differentiate your account management package further? By being bold!

Ideas are scarce. Good ideas are scarcer. As an account manager, you enjoy a lot of privileges. One of them is the right to offer opinions and not having to execute them! Yes, many account managers never quite realize this. If they do, they get too reserved. Their predicament is triggered by the need to be safe than be stupid or the assumption that customers know their turf better. It is true that customers know their battlefield more thoroughly, but it is also true that they are too engrossed in what they are doing that they fail to see what else could be done. They may also be over-conservative.

It is now fashionable for companies to hold 'ideation' sessions, idea retreats, innovation workshops and more to get these instincts into everyday practice. The account manager can add significant value to these processes. Let us see why and how.

How Can Account Managers Participate in This?

First and foremost, account managers are generally well acquainted with the customer's industry and the customer's strengths and weaknesses vis-à-vis other peers. This is fundamental to being an effective account manager, as we have seen earlier. They should also have the knowledge of what industry leaders do, what new products and services they offer and what is their modus operandi or unique propositions. This knowledge can be leveraged to bring forth ideas and suggestions that can impact your customer's brands and businesses. For example, with the knowledge that shoppers in supermarket like to spend more time examining and picking the items but very little time at the checkout counter, a cash register company suggested to its clients to set up an express checkout counter for small number of items. This was implemented in one store initially and is now a universal practice. The idea came from a vendor to the supermarket (based on an end-user insight).

Account managers tend to get too busy with their 'selling' routines that they seldom focus on this opportunity to be of value to the customer. One good idea given and implemented in six months or a year is worth more to a customer than many smart account management steps taken.

One of our medium-sized customers who generally played catch up with large players had a range of soaps which were similar to other leading brands in terms of positioning and the look and feel. The customer was getting frustrated with playing a distant second fiddle to the market leader. In one of our freewheeling discussions, we proposed a new range of products based on fruits—apple, orange and strawberry, among others. No one had this range till then in that market and it could have looked like a questionable idea. You would like to feel fresh after a bath and who would like to end up smelling of apple or orange? (Fruit odors in wash products are not as popular in Asia as in the USA or other western markets.) Yet, we were bold in our advocacy of the idea (as we had seen in some other markets). The customer did not do elaborate consumer research for most of their new ideas. Their strategy was to test market in a controlled market region, observe trial and repeat purchase trends and move on, based on the results. The first range of three products—apple, orange and strawberry—were highly successful in the initial test marketing rounds. The range was extended to grape, raspberry and even lychee. It was nationally launched and even exported. Every two years or so, new fruits were added and the laggards delisted. This kept the brand fresh in consumers' minds. We fragranced about 75% of this customer's products for a very long time. In another instance, we brought the idea (and the recipe and product prototype) of a 'solid scent' to a customer in the Middle East, where summer temperatures and humidity are very high. The solid scent is a good alternative to liquid sprays during such months.

Well-Developed Ideas Maybe Necessary for Some Customers

It is possible that some customers with sophisticated processes may have a different approach to vetting these kinds of 'outsourced' ideas. Account managers may have to do a more thorough homework, brainstorm the ideas internally and perhaps put together market reports in support of their ideas. Many ideas cost nothing, except some good, sequential or lateral thinking and a compelling narrative. All ideas may not be pursued or may not even reach the finish line. However, if you can habituate your customers to accept it from your accounts team, it adds strong credibility in your favor.

As product or service obsolescence sets in many industries rapidly, companies are looking toward blue ocean ideas for business growth. An account manager (and the vendor) is greatly placed to dialogue with their customers in these areas due to their intimacy with the customer's actual business situation (and often that of the whole industry). Ideas can also be offered in other adjacent areas like customers' pricing of products, packaging design, service routines, customer's marketing collateral, merchandising practices, advertising, manufacturing and storage. It is not important just to think of the ideas but to anticipate the questions that may be put to you, articulate the idea to customers, convince them to take it forward and evaluate at the least. The customers are likely to modify your idea based on their own insights, and yet, you can claim credit for your part in that exercise. Account managers who do not exercise this freedom are surrendering a golden opportunity to develop trust, intimacy and shared vision for the customer.

Is it an art to come up with new ideas for your customers? I am not at all convinced that it is. We all get our 'eureka' moment—some do something with it and some let it go waste. One of the internal exercises we did for many customers was to think of a 'brand rejuvenation plan' for struggling brands. This exercise forced us to collect more data, analyze them, prepare a brand health card, compare with their direct competing brands, brainstorm (internally) for ideas, test ideas from elsewhere and write a broad plan to be presented to customers. Bold ideas were encouraged in such exercises. In all instances, these were well received, even if our ideas had not been taken to their logical conclusion.

The next time you visit a Starbucks outlet or a restaurant, observe their processes and see whether you can come up with at least three improvements based on insights that you discover. Even if Starbucks or the restaurant is not your customer, this will prepare you as an account manager to think of your customer's customers and their needs. That is usually a good beginning for new ideas and can develop the ideation instincts gradually.

Success would, however, depend on boldly canvassing such ideas with customers and being prepared to engage in the accompanying conversations. Taking a broad set of ideas to customers is another expression of 'stakeholdership' mindset that customers want to see. The account manager's standing with the customers goes up a few notches. These become little steps to getting close to being considered a customer's advisor.

Account managers may sometimes face situations where the customer is either indifferent to ideas suggested or does not know how to handle them. Gauging the appetite of each customer for new ideas is a skill account managers need to practice. Further, in the case of small and medium customers, it would pay to coach the customer about receiving ideas from vendors and taking them onboard for evaluation. This could be also a value-added service from your company, as such customers may not be privileged recipients of such services from your company or from other vendors.

CHAPTER 8

Pitfalls to Avoid

8.1 DON'T EXPLOIT ROUTES THAT ARE NOT DURABLE OR ETHICAL

Have you been exposed to investigations or allegations of unethical practices? Do your customers or trade practices orient your sales teams toward non-durable tactics? What are the ethical rules of your company and are they indoctrinated into working habits of account teams?

Habits and attitudes matter as much as skills in account management (as in business in general). The moral and ethical question in sales has always been a standard dilemma for many individuals and companies. This is not just a reflection on our moral compass but has a profound effect on long-term customer relationships. Asian (and third world in general) business practices are not always above board. There are indirect buyer-seller collusions, mutual favors, non-transparent deals and even plain cash transfers or expensive gifts like cars, club memberships and holidays. This is quite prevalent in many industries in countries like Korea, China, Vietnam, India, Bangladesh and many African and Latin American countries. It is not important if the customers lead the way in this or vendors deploy it for achieving their short-term benefits. In either case, your company stands to be scrutinized and will perhaps lose.

© The Author(s) 2018
B. Shankar, *Nuanced Account Management*,
https://doi.org/10.1007/978-981-10-8363-1_8

My former company resisted these routes from the very beginning. We may have lost some business in the bargain, but the principle was sacrosanct for us. There is clearly an ethical issue in all these. You may feel the need to do it the wrong way if your product or service does not measure up. If we are confident about our product, service and capabilities of our people, there is just no need to embrace a wrong practice. Such a policy will establish the right value systems for the whole organization and for new recruits.

Some of our large customers in the region were notorious for offering these temptations and would cite stories (both true and fictional) of how other competitors fell in line. Our business with them was pursued only when we both agreed on the transparent conditions of business. The weak salespeople who do not practice account management to its full depth are often the culprits who choose the easy way to secure business. By focusing on a more robust HR policy, we eliminated the need for detoxing salesmen. To us, it was akin to doped players competing with unfair advantage. Our tolerance for any deviation was zero.

One of our best customers with whom we shared a lot, including good value systems, told us at the beginning of our first business that no one in their organization needed to be personally 'taken care of'. The customer went on to ask for a discount from our quoted price to reflect this saving! We were quite taken aback by this direct style. They truly believed (and expected) that every company in the industry was engaged in questionable practices and therefore wanted to draw the line clearly right in the beginning.

The cases of Petrobras, JP Morgan in China, Walmart in India and Toshiba in Japan are too well known to be repeated. Even if some of these are allegations that are yet to be fully proved or disproved, the issues came up to the surface and will sap the energies of these companies (and perhaps their reputation, depending on which way the verdicts go). Corruption and nepotism are more prominent forms of the non-enduring route that I have mentioned.

Mandated Conditions and Regulations

There is a corollary to this aspect. Many customers have stipulated ethical standards that vendors must meet. These could potentially cover not only transactions with them but also general conduct in their businesses. Customers expect and value transparency in all dealings. As reported earlier, this is a potential cause of conflict or defection when breached. Transparency may be defined in the broadest term and the aspects may include pricing, product recommendations, service aspects and so on. We seldom had difficulty with price increase requests, as we provided sufficient verifiable information on the reasons for increases. To some extent, we erred on the side of 'over transparency' with customers.

In several industries (especially banking), regulatory compliance has taken the center stage, following examples of overreach in recent years. Examples like Wells Fargo are chilling demonstration of how far questionable practices in sales can go. Large companies can be extinct (or their reputations severely dented) in days or weeks of information leaks of malpractices. Companies are now forced to declare 'whistle-blower' policies, as corporate governance becomes an increasingly hot-button issue. Sales teams are often at the core of many transgressions in the greed to drive faster growth or manufacture the numbers. It is better to stay on the right side of law and ethics, but that seems as challenging to practice as it is easy to comprehend.

It is often believed that encouragement to do the wrongs comes from the top (either through active abetment or by passive neglect of excesses). Thus sales leaders have to establish the rules and walk the talk. If breaches are discovered, they need to be dealt with exemplary consequences. Business considerations should not impede this attitude.

Here is a list of what you must seek to avoid:

1. Bribes to customers or their agents
2. Favors that are meant to ease your sales
3. Dubious pricing deals
4. Commercial structures that seek to escape government taxes
5. Appointment of personnel without merit for swinging deals
6. Cooking the books (all too familiar now)
7. Selling products or services that offer dubious or fake benefits
8. Clever legal arrangements that seek to circumvent laws.

As a true test of compliance to good ethics, ask yourself if you have turned a blind eye to unethical acts of your account managers in some instances and reflect on what impact it has had on your organization's reputation or on attitude of other colleagues. Even if an act has remained under cover, there is no guarantee that it will not blow up one day.

8.2   DON'T TAKE YOUR EYES OFF COMPETITION

What is the effectiveness of your competition monitoring efforts? Do you have an institutionalized process to ensure regularity, consistency and deep coverage? Is the account team entrusted with the responsibility to own this process and be the pivot for monitoring sales processes and activities of competition?

Are we saying the obvious? Yes and no. B2B businesses tend to have about two–five key comparable competitors in the frame for most opportunities. Some of these companies may not have similar size and capabilities and yet may be fighting in the same arena. Some businesses have even more players, but consolidation constantly moves the field toward a handful of well-resourced companies. Watching competition is a management priority and I am sure most companies do it in their own ways. The intensity and regularity can be erratic depending on how successful a company is. It is therefore possible that when you are meeting all your goals and 'defeating' competition regularly, you may take your eyes off the competition and underestimate their capabilities or miss their new strategies. We may also ignore the fact the competitors may be doing a better job of watching us. As customers develop sophisticated tools to evaluate vendors, companies need to ensure that they can finish well in such evaluations. Many vendor continuity and renewal decisions by customers may be taken based on such periodic evaluation. Furthermore, there is always something new to learn from competition, even if some of them are behind in business terms. The most profitable banks, for instance, are in the midscale category and not in the mega-league. They must be doing something right. Depending on the scope of your business, the relevant competition could be global, thus requiring a global watch.

Gary Hamel and C.K. Prahalad,[1] in their seminal book, postulated three types of competition (watch): product-market competition, competition to foreshorten migration paths and competition on industry leadership. We refer to the first one, namely 'product-market competition' here. This is a short-term activity to be vested with the account and sales teams

---

[1] Gary Hamel and C.K. Prahalad, *Competing for the future*, (Harvard Business School press, 1994).

to track on a continuous basis. (As would be evident, the other forms mentioned are more medium to long term, involving a larger team of managers and analysts.)

Three Dimensions to Watch

We monitored competition on at least three dimensions—structure, strategy and staff (besides the usual operational or 'daily' tactics). We were keen to understand each competitor's strategy for each large customer and used different sources of information to collate the strategy. The sources included our customers, other competitors, our suppliers, industry experts and, of course, secondary sources of information. It is very useful to know if a competitor is adopting an all-out pricing strategy or a 'low' customization strategy or a full-service strategy or a strategy focused only on higher value products or high potential customers and so on. If done well, this helps in providing a clear view of the landscape with each key customer or customer segments. We were also keenly monitoring the profile, caliber and style of account managers from competition, due to the importance we placed on that role. Account management was our clear competitive advantage, and we did not want to be left behind if the race was turning hotter. It wasn't so much of keeping a tab on competitive 'tricks' but a desire to benchmark with best practices, wherever they existed. Once a year, we had a formal competitor analysis over a vast majority of areas, including competitor's major successes and failures, people changes, service package, financial insights, strategy shifts, new strengths, investments, among others. The account managers were the antennas through which the information flowed to our company. They would present periodically their assessment of competition and implications for our company. Once trained to be competent, account teams enjoy this exercise.

A key reason for our early successes in several markets was the finding that our competitors offered their full service to multinational clients but their services were often abridged for local and regional customers, some of whom were as big as multinational players in specific markets. In markets like India, Indonesia, Thailand, China, Korea and Bangladesh, the local players as a cluster were larger than multinationals in market share terms. We used the insight to step up our service levels for some key local customers and provided a compelling point of difference. In several cases, we enjoyed greater than normal share of the wallet (50% and above) and for a sustained period of time. This was based on extending our stakeholder attitude to these customers and working toward their market share and brand goals. Our competitors did catch up with us when some multinational businesses started to dry up and thus we had to be watchful even more when our success rate was higher and invited more competitive scrutiny.

Sources of Competitive Analysis

Unlike the B2C situation where marketing strategies are more visible by the actions in the marketplace, which can easily be tracked, a B2B competition study needs to be based on some facts and some intelligent inferences. Information that is readily available may be sketchy with gaps but experienced account teams can connect the dots to derive plausible scenarios. Account managers and other managers involved in the exercise need to be given such exposure. In my coaching experiences, I have discovered that salesmen tend to stop at watching day-to-day operational tactics of competitors (price quotes, who visits customers from competition, some solution proposals, dates of events and meetings, wins or losses) and do not always have the skill to go beyond, to the strategic level or competent enough to formulate response strategies. They also do not do this as a conscious activity, either because of lack of time or due to such activities being assigned to a 'strategy department' who may be removed from the marketplace realities. This is where the role of the account manager and sensitizing them to the importance comes in. Some knowledge of financial analysis, basic SWOT analysis or some other competitive analysis framework is useful for account managers. Account managers often rise up the ladder to head businesses or geographies and this learning is critical for effective performance of those higher roles. One way to expose them to this would be to rotate them to jobs in strategic or category management departments for some period of time. It is an easier way of providing the knowledge, the tools and the interpretation skills.

In companies where competition watch is a corporate activity (due to factors that go beyond the account team), it often remains in the domain of senior management and account managers seldom see the gist of what they need to know. In such situations, there must be a mechanism of sharing the relevant parts of these analyses.

For your top 10 or 20 customers, draw up a table of strategies employed by your next biggest competitor(s), the differentiators (technology or marketing advantages, people strengths, etc.) and current thrust areas. Compare this with what you are doing or your company is involved with and derive a gap analysis. You may wish to close some gaps or may not be able to close them, but being aware is the first step to fine-tune your position with those key customers.

8.3   Don't Ignore New Competition

Are you in an industry where new competitors keep walking in regularly? Do you have a professional mechanism to track them and their methods and strategies? Do you face situations when a smart new competitor has already made inroads into your business or potential? Are your account managers guilty of ignoring the threat of new competitors?

I think it is harder to be a market leader than a market challenger.—Philip Kotler, legendary pioneer of marketing concepts

What is common to Amazon, Tesla, Genentech, Huawei, Alliance Data Systems and Spirit AeroSystems? They are now Fortune 500 companies (or on the fringe) but were hardly noticed when they started out. New competition is deliberately presented in this book as a new chapter, distinct from ignoring or watching the regular competitors. Michael Porter of Harvard Business School had in fact included 'threat of new competition' as one of the five forces in his epoch concept, 'the five forces analysis'. The characteristics of new competitors are often different.

How Do New Competitors Differ?

1. They are plain hungrier for business and survival.
2. They are often smaller but nimble (start-ups).
3. They employ different tactics than what is common in the industry (online marketing, for example).
4. They may focus on one or two opportunities or segments or needs (fintech).
5. They may have lower overheads and can follow an aggressive pricing (or freebies) strategy (happens frequently in industrial equipment).
6. They are eager and hence tend to offer high-touch and personalized service levels (building or electrical contractors).

7. They spend disproportionate resources on one or two first clients in order to get entry and use that as marketing leverage (common in most industries).
8. They may 'poach' people from more established competitors in order to ramp up learning and go-to-market speeds.
9. They may also be successful in hiring top talents by offering start-up experience and stakes in the company. These are good attractions among the millennials.
10. Their products may be more advanced as they do not get bogged down with existing designs or tools or legacy technologies.
11. They tend to think in discontinuities rather than incremental shifts (salesforce.com).
12. They may offer free-trial packages in order to induce trials.
13. They may tailor commercial terms to the needs of every customer.
14. The lean organization set up allows them shorter turnarounds for changes to product designs, services.
15. They are often the first to embrace new business models that may impress customers (Uber, eBay).
16. New competitors offer quick deliveries after purchase as a differentiator.
17. They may outsource more areas in order to shorten the cycle of product or service development. They don't feel constrained because of sunken in-house resources, unlike established players.
18. New companies will offer to do significant tailoring, which existing ones resist.
19. New companies may offer 'no questions asked returns' in order to induce buyers—obviously most older companies will try to keep away from such tactics (Zappos.com).
20. New companies may be happier to have market shares or subscriber base in the first phase of their development instead of strict financial goals.
21. They also attract a lot of venture capital (VC) funds, which eases their developmental pangs, leaving them to concentrate on getting their product or service out quickly and on developing customer relationships.
22. Customers may love their less bureaucratic and decision-making style

Given these substantial scope for disruptive 'behavior', it is vital for vendors and their account managers to spot these competitors and to initiate formal tracking of their strategies and activities. This can be rendered difficult sometimes, as these players often operate 'below the radar'. Their flexibility with almost everything could throw you off guard. In fact, this has already gotten a buzzword: '*Agile Marketing*'. It was recently reported that only 43% of the Fortune 500 companies that existed 20 years ago have retained their membership of the club! That is an unbelievable influx of new players, in only 20 years. These companies must have had a surreptitious start that ballooned into massive enterprises in their industry space.

New competition also often creates new premise of competitive advantage. Would you think of 'humor' as one? That's what this company did (albeit in the consumer space): 'Interestingly, competing for and winning on the humor dimensions have proven successful. To illustrate, the German electronics retail giant MediaMarkt focuses on being humorous and funny. The company is neither the cheapest nor the one with the best stores or locations. However, its positioning of being the "funniest" has contributed to its market leadership position as consumers arrive in hordes. In short, "soft issues" such as humor or design may amount to an important source of competitive advantage in the future—a stark contrast to traditional sources of competitive advantage such as low cost and quality.'[2]

> New competitors are becoming more numerous, more formidable, and more global—and some destroy more value for incumbents than they create for themselves.[3]

Window of Entry for New Vendors
One key question is: Why would B2B customers entertain a 'new' player? It is true that many customers in many industries have long established 'rigid' protocols for dealing with vendors. Many have preferred vendors and do not deal outside the arrangement. Loyalty is another stubborn factor. Some expect stringent conditions to be fulfilled before a new player is even allowed at the entry point. Yet, companies are often curious to listen to new vendors, especially where there is a strong technology angle or where the new company is led

---

[2] Oliver Heil, Don Lehmann and Stefan Stremersch, *Marketing competition in the 21st century* (*International Journal of Research in Marketing*, Vol. 27, Issue 2, 2010), 161–163.

[3] *Playing to win: The new global competition for corporate profits* (McKinsey Global Institute, September 2015).

by an accomplished industry veteran or when the new company's marketing promise is different and exciting. Some customers who operate at the cutting edge have a window for new vendors to come in if they have new ideas. This window is created to make sure that such new ideas can help them launch pioneering products from their stable. Companies regard the encouragement to new or start-up outfits as a ticket to innovation and the future. Further, companies can sometimes salivate at the prospect of better prices for what they buy, especially where the product specifications do not vary much and when the industry goes through difficult times. This is the success mantra for late entrants like Asus into the enterprise computing segment. In fact, most companies have a goal known as 'vendor development' for their purchasing and technical group. Under this, companies would actually encourage promising small players, with resource support and promise of trials, to accelerate their product or service development cycles, in their own interest. All of these should be encouraging to you if you are a David challenging Goliath.

It is thus a no-brainer that smaller or newer competitors cannot be ignored. While tracking such new players, account managers need to make a realistic assessment of where these companies could make an impact, what will be the type of impact and when the threat will cross the danger line. Account managers could be guilty of not just ignoring the existence of such new competitors but also underplaying their advances due to lack of good tracking mechanism.

Surprising Established Competition

When we started our fragrance business in India in the 1990s, we were a good 15–20 years behind the key global players in that market. We were the underdogs for the initial couple of years. We used this to our advantage to focus on maybe about five customers, study their brands in detail (strengths and weaknesses) and pick the best approach to make the first move. In one case, we made contact directly with the owner team, and in another, we went through the technical team (offering technical solutions to persistent problems). In another case, we offered trial quantities free of cost. In a fourth case of a local small player (now a dominant no. 3 in the market), we approached both the owner and his primitive product development department offering them help in formulating products. All these approaches were carefully chosen after studying the entry barriers. All our account managers including me (I headed the country operations) were industry outsiders and therefore most of the industry perhaps couldn't fathom how we would succeed. Further, our company was globally ranked about the seventh and that didn't give us any unique ammunition to peddle.

Our approach, as a 'new' entrant thus consisted of the following, among other things:

- Careful choice and management of contact and entry point
- Choosing relatively easier targets for businesses at the early stage (for example, local brands than that of multinationals)
- Account managers from outside the industry, with fresh perspectives
- Initial customer contacts steered by senior experienced people
- Focus limited to a few customers, chosen by us
- Working on a clear account plan
- Differentiating on service as product differentiation was difficult
- Extensive homework on customer brands, analysis and insights
- Not only working on official projects but also proposing new projects addressing customer's problems
- Different 'sales' pitch to different customers (storytelling and adaptation)
- Demonstrating sharper understanding of customer needs
- Quick turnarounds of product iterations, trials
- Extremely close and vigilant follow-up with customers
- Tight internal progress reviews and frequent drawing up of action plans
- Being prepared with a Plan B in all situations
- Demonstrating operating flexibility wherever required (and valued)

None of this seems like rocket science for any vendor. But that's precisely the point—that old vendors become too conservative and set in their ways, offering critical openings for the newcomers. Whilst we were making good progress with all the initially prioritized customers, the competition ignored us and for very long. Our support team in the Asia Pacific headquarters understood the golden opportunity that we had in a new market and dramatically ramped up their support, turnaround times, quality and engagement of senior people. Once the first five customers became buyers, it was quite easy for us to approach other customers, including multinationals, who came with higher degrees of entry difficulties. Our success rate resulted in an 18% market share in India, outpacing everybody else in the market. This was achieved in about six–seven years. It was not a flash in the pan, as over the next 15 years or so, the company has maintained its mid-teen shares in a rapidly expanding market. Competition has, of course, caught up as well, but the early gains and the effective implementation of account management are solid enough to sustain themselves over the long haul.

The Modern Day Davids in Corporate World
The 'fintech', 'medtech' and SMAC (social media analytics companies) industries have several such stories. Majors like Oracle, SAP, Google, Microsoft and pharma and technology giants have been busy tracking these start-ups, not merely to watch their competitive ploys but to acquire them at the right time and before the others did. It is an indirect acknowledgment that these start-ups have redefined the rules of the game and succeeded despite the large incumbents. They reckon that their own organization, vested with vast resources, may not be able to find or create such opportunities and solutions with ingenuity and alacrity. Tesla in the car industry is another such example and so is Amazon. The internet has been a great leveler. In many industries, it has been possible for start-ups to zoom quickly, by non-conventional approaches to design, development and analysis of user needs. Technology is not the only disruptor. Business models too. This trend is bound to continue.

Whether your business is an old-fashioned 'biggies' play zone or a modern tech field that draws upon the power of the internet, you must actively watch out for smart new competitors. In the B2B industries, new competitors may take time to record their first business in order terms but may have encroached many months before, into the activity cycle, unnoticed.

Identify ten players who could be your potential competitors and analyze their strengths, weaknesses, competitive positioning and areas of first attacks. With better monitoring, you may be able to prune the list to the three or four who must be watched very closely. Every year that you ignore them, they are stealing your market share gradually and making unnoticed entry into key customers.

8.4   DON'T ALLOW POLITICS TO OVERSHADOW GOOD ACCOUNT MANAGEMENT

Is the politics within your account and support teams acting as an impediment to your progress with customer projects? Are there cross purposes that are frequently at play? Does any member(s) have an agenda that is different from your account management goals? Do sales leaders in your organization feel helpless in reining in politics?

Politics in organizations was born when organizations were born. Inter-departmental rivalry is a constant unspoken devil in many companies. It stems from both divergent individual aspirations and tangential departmental goals (and ego clashes). The inherent conflicts manifest with political overtones. This behavior is the antithesis of a successful account management program. We have seen that successful account management is founded on good team play and complementary performances by various staff. No single person will deliver all the goals over a sustained period. The technical team, for instance, may pour cold water on an exciting sales prospect on the grounds that it has unrealistic expectations, even without examining if expectations could be modified or dealt with in multiple steps. A customer likes to deal with an organization that seems well oiled, works seamlessly, is well informed across the board, shows the same degree of attention, commitment and care for the customer, displays unity and does not bring rivalry into customer meetings. It devolves on the leader of the team to keep the working of the organization above such petty indulgences or professional quarrels.

In our context, two conflicts were common and both had some political undertones. Salesmen were sometimes challenged by the creative team on realism (with respect to customer projects—project objective vs. cost or time or inconsistency with brand and consumer). This could lead to good projects being thrown out the window unless arbitrated effectively. Similarly, product evaluators or scent design managers who chose or short-listed fragrances were under pressure from the creative team while they shortlisted products from the choices made available by the creative team. These conflicts had to be managed, without boiling over, as everyone was keen to have a share in the potential sweepstakes.

As B2B businesses tend to last many years, if not decades, it is also conceivable that different generations of account teams try to show their predecessor teams in poor light. This does not help to score any valuable point with the customer. Instead, it may brand your company as an unprofessional entity and could jeopardize further opportunities. We made sure that account managers were sensitive to this and references to previous teams were always respectful even when old contracts, in hindsight, were discovered to be unfavorable to the company.

Cross-functional disagreements (which many times take political overtones) were kept out of customer discussions and account managers tackled issues only as organizational representatives. These points may seem elementary, but given the long duration of the relationship, multiple players in the processes and the human need for egos to be massaged, it can be a precarious political balance and thus needs careful observance. As every activity in front of a customer cannot be monitored, the failsafe option is to train the account managers and for leaders to act as role models in shaping collegial behavior that clearly projects the organizational interests.

The culture of an organization provides the thread for individual and collective behavior. An organization full of rules where each individual has to fend for his supper is potentially a war-zone, as account managers and support teams look for opportunities to outscore each other. On the other hand, an organization with less rules but one that has enduring values promotes collective effort. The values run as undercurrents in group and in individual behavior. It is thus important to spend a lot of energy and effort in building the right culture that fosters group optimization, resulting in less political wars. Even if it is arduous to build this for the whole organization, smaller account teams (country team, divisional team, etc.) could embrace such ethos. The responsibility for this lies squarely on the account team leaders. In our context, we emphasized on collective ownership of final outcomes, not just on paper, but by real-time inspirational 'walk the talk' leadership and direction. Scope for schisms was thus kept really low.

Organizations sport inherent fault lines—marketing versus sales, R&D versus marketing, finance versus sales, regulatory versus business development, design versus marketing and so on. Departmental goals and incentives may work against each other, even if unwittingly. Politics and blame game can also raise their heads when things go wrong.

If your company would like to make a beginning to streamline this, start with identifying potential conflicts or areas of disagreement and lay down guidelines for dealing with them. Such guidelines should include the recommended solution and how to deal with the aftermath, in case political flashes surface. A tricky question: How would you deal with a highly successful account manager who is also very political? (Clue: organization is greater than individuals.)

CHAPTER 9

The Payoff and Concluding Chapters

9.1 THE PAYOFF

Account management is not merely a sales approach or strategy. It should now be clear from the foregoing chapters that it is a culture and a way of life. Sales teams and all other functions supporting them are symbiotic elements of this cultural notion. For salesmen, it is a paradigm change in the 'state of the mind'. The many facets of it enumerated in the book take time to build and refine. They need strong commitment from the top and perseverance from all. That is perhaps why not many companies have quite embraced the philosophy to the full extent. It needs a shared vision among key stakeholders in the company and a clear road map to develop it gradually and embed into all processes and actions of people. The practice gets perfected by two things: (1) repeated application of the methods, every day and (2) a few account managers becoming so good in the act, as to excel as role models. In an ideal scenario, it is also useful to share the framework with customers in order to derive its full advantages and to set clear expectations from both sides. A 'high-touch approach' based customer engagement is not every customer's natural demand. It may need to be sold in some situations, citing the enormous benefits that they can derive. Thus the 'account management promise' to a customer can crown your product and service offerings.

A good parallel to quote in the consumer world is the 'Disney experience'. Early visitors to Disneyland had some idea of what fun to expect, but no clue of the service standards. Walt Disney created his own paradigm and

© The Author(s) 2018
B. Shankar, *Nuanced Account Management*,
https://doi.org/10.1007/978-981-10-8363-1_9

standardized its delivery. He also built in a virtuous cycle of improvements that kept raising the bar in terms of process, people and outcomes. Today the Disney customer experience is taught in training programs.

A good account management system is no different. The payoff from a well-implemented high-performance nuanced account management system is immense. From higher revenues, profits to loyalty, stability, longevity of businesses to professional quality of trained people and, most importantly, a sustainable model that goes beyond generations of people on both sides of the aisle. The unquantifiable outcome of a well-run account management program can also be seen in customer-supplier bonds and in their cozy ecosystem. This is the ultimate destination. The collective model can also be source of great competitive advantage not easily replicable. Companies have also benefitted by being able to attract high quality and stable talent, arising from excellent account management practices.

The scope and breadth of account management is almost infinite. There is really no beginning or end to the set of activities that is in this realm. In some respects, it is comparable to the responsibilities a parent has toward his or her child. If implemented well, it neutralizes the pitfalls of 'silo' working that tends to create too many seams in organizations. A well-bred account manager metamorphoses into an account leader and a coach.

The competitive advantage spectrum has evolved steadily from product differentiation to service differentiation to IT-led process enablers to partnerships and blue ocean strategies. The quest will continue. In a world of increasing and unexpected competitive threats, this 'soft power' can prove to be a sustainable competitive advantage and a powerful gateway for the stakeholder relationship that customers seek. The vast scope of account management strategies and tools also provides several avenues across the various touchpoints for continuous innovation depending upon the current level of excellence attained by vendors. Innovation in processes and practices are hard to copy and offer the potential to be your unique selling proposition for a long time.

Challenges Ahead

Even though implementation of such a process change is not always a 180-degree turn, it can face a number of challenges:

1. As with any change, it shakes up the existing system and those reveling in it will feel apprehensive (especially heroes or solitary salesmen).
2. It can lead to changes to your strategies (target customers, targeted outcomes, timelines, product or service portfolio, sales targets).
3. It needs significant unlearning, relearning in processes and customer interface approaches. Salesmen's brain may need to be rewired to some extent.
4. It will need enormous training and reorientation of people to the new roles and capabilities.
5. It will change the organization structure and can affect people (who may not fit into the new role definitions).
6. It calls for changes in the way senior management interact with and mentor sales teams.
7. It needs some investments at the start (new people, new processes and systems, training).
8. It needs persistence, discipline and teamwork like all major tasks associated with change.
9. It may need to be explained to customers who may have been used to a different style of engagement from you.
10. It may need big changes in aspects like salesmen performance measurement and their compensation.
11. It will be regularly challenged by the 'naysayers' especially if the results are slow to come.

The introductory and the follow-up phases have to be managed carefully in order to cope with these challenges smoothly. As with other organizational changes, it will need special task forces, champions, unwavering commitment from the top management and nurturing. Depending upon the organization and the current state of deployment of one or more of the principles, the full scope of nuanced account management, even in evolved organizations, is clearly a three–five years' process, but the trophies are bound to come home. The good part of this is that account management can be implemented in steps or phases, as the adoption matures gradually.

9.2   Account Organization

Based on the reasonable assumption that you are convinced about the fit between account management strategic vision and your needs, we will explore some preparatory steps. The key to implementing a nuanced account management framework is to create an account organization. This organization should be treated as an 'evolving' apparatus that centers around the strengths of the company, the needs of the customers and successes achieved with implementation of the account management concept at different stages. There are several issues that impact the building up of an effective account organization. We have seen some of them in the earlier paragraphs. In this chapter, we will discuss considerations and possible frameworks. We make a conscious assumption here that account organizations may differ from customer to customer for the same vendor in order to account for differences in the customer nature, type or buying behavior. There are also situations wherein the customer could dictate the size and composition of your account organization.

The structure of an account organization flows directly from your goals for the customer. These goals include revenue metrics, profitability metrics, service metrics, share of wallet objectives, the relative ranking you seek with the customer (top supplier, among the top three suppliers, etc.) and the relative importance of the customer (as dictated by company's choice). Structural considerations will vary, for instance, desire for the customer to be one of your top five revenue or profit contributors vis-à-vis a mid-level target. It is not necessary that all 'large' buyers will be in the top group of customers for a vendor. Companies will adopt different segmentation rules based on their own criteria. (Segmentation is a topic by itself and widely covered in marketing literature.)

Considerations for Setting Up the Organization

Account organizations must reckon with the following additional considerations:

- *Scope* and nature of tasks (pre-sales effort, post-sales servicing, technical support, commercial and legal negotiations)
- *Frequency* of customer *contacts* (operating level, management level)
- Levels, number and *seniority* of customer managers involved in the engagement
- *Skills* required in addition to standard sales skills (data mining and analysis, strategic perspective, customer training, legal correspondence, video or audio productions, financial calculations like IRR)
- *Bandwidth* considerations for each account managers vis-à-vis the breadth and depth of tasks to be performed

- *Tenure* of the engagement plan (five years, ten years, etc.). It could also be perpetual.
- *Support functions* required as complements (R&D, product development, patent expertise, fundamental scientific expertise, market research, brand management, tendering)
- *Regional and global scope* (of the vendor and the customer)
- *Industry practice* (and the maturity of account management concept in the industry). It is not necessary to follow the industry practice except for basic elements.
- *Automation and technology* dynamics in the market or the industry (portals, end-to-end shared digital spaces, online transaction ability)
- Available caliber of *people* (this could change over time)
- *Implementation strategy* (all customers together or in phases)

Four Generic Types of Account Organizations

Based on the importance of the customer and all the above factors, four structural options can be evaluated (refer Fig. 9.1):

1. At a simple level, one 'dedicated' account manager for a customer, supported by an account administrative team. All support functions are common for the customer or a group of customers or for a geography. This structure is adopted usually for local/national customers, without any regional or global scope and for medium-sized customers.

Fig. 9.1   Account management organization types

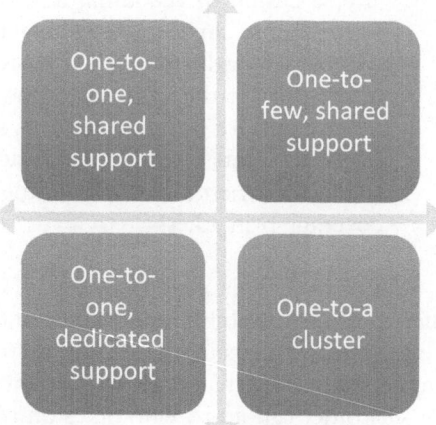

2. A group of 'dedicated' account managers (maybe two to five) depending on the size and businesses of the customer, supported by an administrative team. The support functions may or may not be dedicated. This approach is useful where the customer has several divisions (Dial, Siemens, for example) and while some common principles of engagement apply, each division has different requirements and may even have a different buying process or philosophy or buyers. One of the account managers can assume the coordination role.

3. The third structure is more complex. Besides dedicated account managers (in different geographies based on the reach) and an administrative team, there would be dedicated support functions as well—R&D, market research, product development and so on. Customers like GE, Walmart, Unilever, Pepsi and P&G will fall into this category for most vendors and may expect or demand something like this. Due to the size and complexity of this structure, there is usually a head called as 'Account Director' or 'Global Account Head', whose responsibility is to helm the relationship seamlessly across functions and geographies, based on a unified strategy and approach on the ground. The heads of this complex structure are typically very senior executives, with C-level exposure and, most certainly, with significant account management experience. Some of the global account heads may even rank above some divisional or business heads, owing to the importance of the customer.

4. In smaller companies (or with small/medium-sized customers), it is also common to find 'non-dedicated' account managers, who look after a clutch of accounts, linked either by geography or industry. For example, an account manager of an adhesive company may deal with all the industrial OEM customers or with all customers in the north-east. If there are common buying variables or homogenous buying culture or language, this structure is very appropriate. How many accounts to attach to an account manager would depend on the factors mentioned above, the load factor, optimum service and coverage principles?

Wherever there is a group or a team in the account organization, a clear charter of responsibilities and accountabilities accompanies the structure. This is critical to ensure that things do not fall through any cracks. It is also important to note that in all the scenarios, there is at least 'one' person that the customer can go to who takes on the role of the orchestra conductor.

This is fundamentally different from conventional sales organizations, where customers may buy from an organization or from a department or a phone salesperson or an email salesperson, in all cases, faceless entities. That is not the only difference. Going by the arguments of all the previous chapters, there is perhaps a more significant variance in the 'process' and 'practice' of selling that is a signature of account management. The strategies, process and practice are perhaps bigger and trickier pieces of the puzzle.

Another notable departure from a traditional sales set-up is the fact that account organizations are (generally) hierarchically flat. The account managers, their seniors and support functional managers act as colleagues at the same level, as far as the customer is concerned. It is possible that they carry varying levels of authority for decision-making within the vendor organization, though. The account team heads usually hold a high office in an organization, reporting either to the CEO or to the head of the division (in case of multi-business enterprises).

One important conundrum organizations face is how to mesh the account management structure with the rest of the organization, which may be organized on functional lines or geographical lines or a combination. For example, what is the connection between a dedicated R&D resource person of a large account and the company's corporate R&D? The dotted relationship concept comes to the rescue. However, this is not without potential for confusion. Aligning objectives, resources, setting project priorities, measuring outcomes and rewarding people could pose a lot of confusion, if not structured well. One solution is to have a support manager as part of the corporate team but on loan to an account management group. In this arrangement, cost and time are apportioned to the account and expertise is drawn from the corporate group. It is advisable to make these relationships and connections formal in order to avoid conflicts.

The other key aspect accountants will tell you about is how much it costs to set up these account organizations and what is the payback. A dedicated account team, whatever is its size, costs a lot more than shared resources. In the B2B context, the investment in teams and their activities precede results by many months or years. Thus, it is a serious commitment that the top management has to consciously decide on. Some companies adopt a gradual build-up plan for their account organizations, to align with the pace of activities and interest shown by the customer. This will naturally ensure a more progressive cost structure. Each situation is different and will need a specific account organization plan.

9.3   Account Management Implementation Road Map

Companies may be at the start of examining an account management system (this book has hopefully nudged you to think seriously about launching it) or may have a reasonably matured deployment. For the former type who wishes to usher in account management, the following six-step model implementation plan offers a template and key steps centered around six platforms (see Fig. 9.2).

Foundation

- Segmentation of customers/formation of customer clusters for the different businesses (in case of a multi-business organization). It is advisable to segment customers into four or five groups.
- Choice of which customers to extend full account management concept (perhaps prudent to start with a small list to gain experience)
- Study of account management practices in the industry (especially serving the same customer lists as your company)

Design

- The full scope of what account management in your company will entail—tasks, activities, outcomes
- A blueprint of services to be offered to different clusters of customers (customization, product or service minimum tenures, after-sales support, advisory services, special pricing terms, other privileges, etc.). Where a partial account management service is to be adopted (for certain customers), the abridged scope to be clearly defined (what is in, what is out).

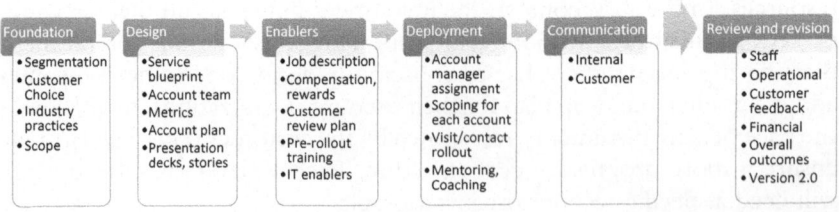

Fig. 9.2   Account implementation plan template

- Form account teams (refer to Sect. 9.2 on account organization for models) and the structure.
- Decide metrics for measurement—client level, account manager level, team level, business level, company level and so on
- Account plan preparation for each account with goals, strategies and action plans. If intermediate and long terms goals and strategies differ, a separate plan for the respective time horizons is advised.
- Prepare standard company presentation decks—credentials, strengths, weaknesses, product or service offerings, organization structure, strategic focus and all standard information and charts. Multiple sets for different types/clusters of customers and use of modern technologies and tools are recommended.
- Question bank for opportunities/projects commencement (may include project forms or templates) to standardize information gathering.
- Templates for customer communication, meeting minutes, price quotations, contracts, sales orders

Enablers

- Job description of account manager and other support managers (basis: develop roles and responsibilities from all the previous chapters)
- Operating guidelines—dos and don'ts, authority, consultation and decision routines
- Decision on changes to account team and support team compensation, incentives, rewards and recognition
- Pre-rollout training and orientation for account teams and support teams
- Internal review frequencies and formats
- Customer review frequency, format, parameters and attendees
- Development of IT enablers—data capture, analysis, project tracking, alerts, web and online capabilities and so on

Deployment

- Assignment of accounts to account managers (a very vital task based on fit, capability of individual vs. account complexity and importance, readiness for the role)

- Hire new account managers (and support managers) if necessary.
- Scope of activity coverage for each account—prospecting, pre-sales, sales, post-sales, other supporting services, special privileges
- Mentoring, on-the-job coaching (by role model managers)
- Rollout of visit/contact plan and deployment for each account.

Communication

- Internal communication to all staff and account teams—explanation of the concept, roles, performance expectations, outcome expectations, rewards and so on (preferably in several media).
- Communication to chosen customers on what they could expect from the account management deployment, how the system will work, feedback and review mechanisms, roles and expectations of people on both sides.

Review and Revision

- First review workshop—financial, project, account, account manager level analysis of efforts, results achieved, challenges faced, success stories—a good review point will be six months after deployment.
- Staff reviews (suitability to the role, alignment to types of customers, performance with customers, customer feedback, speed of learning, overall effectiveness, extent of concept application)
- Detailed operational review of systems, processes and procedures—what works and what does not?
- Customer feedback on the effectiveness of the deployed system, pros and cons, areas for improvement, ratings for the company and the account teams.
- Financial analysis of top-line results, profitability and account management costs (additional).
- Management analysis of efficacy of the account management system and approach (12 months after implementation).
- Recognition for early results (to motivate and direct behavior towards stronger embrace).
- Preparation of version 2.0 incorporating changes, fine-tunes and extensions.

As with any new system or process, everything may not fall into place quickly. Customization and fine-tuning with early experiences is important to ensure that the system is appropriate, responsive and within the implementation capability of the organization. Account teams and customers must be encouraged to provide constant feedback until a steady state can be reached. A core implementation group with the necessary skills and training will smoothen the adoption of the system. The system needs nurturing (and patience) from top management too and diligent documentation from all concerned. A well-implemented system would justify itself in the form of better commercial outcomes, longevity and depth of customer engagement. All of these are measurable at every stage of implementation. They should also correlate to a strong customer feedback.

Early Dividends

Some of the early potential dividends are as follows:

- Account teams are spending more time with priority customers (and with the right people).
- You are getting more enquiries and projects from customers whose share of wallet you want to improve.
- Customers are demanding more services from you (contrary to normal instinct, this is a good development). Only if you are a desirable supplier, you will get such demands.
- You get positive customer feedback and encouragement, unsolicited.
- Your account manager gets invited to sit in some internal meetings of your customers.
- You get a second or third try in a given project.
- You get invited to make presentations at an early stage of a project.
- You are able to secure some difficult appointments with customers.
- Your informal reach in the customer is improving (more contacts, more conversations, more communication).
- Your project pipeline is growing strongly (percent growth in project dollars much higher than previous periods).
- You can feel a greater amount of buzz among the account managers and the support teams.
- You can sense a greater vigil from your competitors.

Make sure that your system tracks such encouraging developments early. It is good for the morale of the team and a fillip to the implementation. The early promise can also be leveraged to secure additional resources for account management (people, space, digital investments, technical resources, capability enhancement projects). Organizations that embark on account management will also need to redraw their core business goals and strategies based on the outcomes achieved. For example, if the deployment is successful, it will lead to a greater share of wallet with some customers, directly contributing to revenue growth. Equally, the account management scope may require enhancement and extension (to more customers or additional services), impacting cost structures and people decisions. If you are faced with such positive dynamics, it must bode well for your business and that you are well on your way!

INDEX[1]

---

[1] Note: Page numbers followed by 'n' refer to notes.

© The Author(s) 2018
B. Shankar, *Nuanced Account Management*,
https://doi.org/10.1007/978-981-10-8363-1